6. <u>00</u>

D1450760

THE SUPERMARKET

THE SUPERMARKET:
AN ANALYSIS OF GROWTH,
DEVELOPMENT, AND CHANGE

REVISED EDITION

ROM J. MARKIN
Associate Professor of Business Administration
Washington State University

WASHINGTON STATE UNIVERSITY PRESS
1968

Printed in the United States of America as a publication
of the Bureau of Economic and Business Research,
Washington State University, Pullman, Washington.

PREFACE TO THE REVISED EDITION

The supermarket is one of America's pace-setting retailing institutions. Furthermore, it is uniquely an American invention— another of the myriad examples of what was once called "Yankee ingenuity." In addition, this American institution, which has streamlined the retail distribution of food and related items, has been widely adopted abroad and has, to a considerable extent, been regarded as the "model" of retail merchandising efficiency in many other countries as well as in the United States. Although it was unknown 40 years ago, the supermarket is today the dominant outlet for food as well as an important source for many other nonfood consumer items.

The basic ingredients of supermarket merchandising remain today, essentially those of the early supers—the cash and carry and self-service stores—that operated from the 1930's through the 1950's. These earlier efforts were described and analyzed in the first edition of this study. However, during the 1960's there have been many new and interesting variations in retail food merchandising. The revised edition of this book is an effort to chronicle and analyze these many variations and to assess their importance in terms of present and future supermarket strategy and policy.

The revised edition, as was the earlier study, is designed and directed to a broad audience. The point of view is largely managerial. I hope that food marketing executives and those who aspire to managerial and executive positions will benefit from the study. Food distribution personnel and those in related industries who desire to be well informed on food marketing developments also may find it useful. Management trainees and marketing students at the college level, as well as academicians who are interested in institutional developments at all levels of retail distribution, are likely to find their interaction with this study meaningful.

As is the usual case, I am indebted to many for their valuable assistance in helping me to undertake this revision. First of all, my gratitude for a remarkable trade literature is boundless. Such literature makes possible the ideal climate for communication and information. The trade literature is so extensive that individual mention would indeed be an Olympian task.

My learned colleague from the University of Idaho, Professor Russell Chrysler, did a meticulous and critical job in reviewing the drafts of the revised edition and made valuable suggestions for improvement in both organization and content.

Roger Decker, my industrious and intelligent graduate assistant, did yeoman service in ferreting out valuable research material from the labyrinthine structure referred to on most university campuses as the library.

I am indebted to Professor John A. Guthrie, Director of the Washington State University Bureau of Economic and Business Research, for encouraging me and for underwriting the effort with a summer research grant. His cooperation, along with the secretarial and editorial assistance of Mrs. Glenda Boone and Mrs. Anna Campbell, made a heavy task much less burdensome.

Finally, as are most married men, I am indebted to my wife, Mitzi, who throughout the summer of 1967 armed me each morning with a cup of coffee and a gentle admonishment to "stay with it," as she pushed me into my home study.

ROM J. MARKIN
January, 1968

CONTENTS

TABLES

FIGURES

Chapter 1 | Introduction

FOOD RETAILING is America's largest retail business. For the twenty-sixth consecutive year, retail food sales reached an all-time peak and have now exceeded $70 billion in annual sales volume. What is the nature and character of America's largest, and perhaps most complex, retail business? What are the factors and forces that have led to the phenomenal development and growth of supermarkets in the postwar period? Why is the supermarket frequently characterized as America's most efficient retail distributor? These are but a few of the many fascinating, if not perplexing, questions which concern retail food store marketing and which appear greatly in need of analysis.

Growth, development, and change in retail food store distribution in the post-World War II period have been little short of phenomenal. Of the total volume of retail food store business in 1966, the supermarket accounted for 71.3 and the superette for 12.8 per cent. The remaining 15.9 per cent was achieved by the category designated small stores.[1] The overwhelming dominance and importance of the supermarket in the retail food industry is certainly dramatized by these statistics.

A few other statistics and developments are no less intriguing.

Immediately following World War II, during the decade 1948-1958, grocery store sales far outran population growth and increases in per capita income. For the same period, expenses (wages, rent, heat, light, and promotional) were greater, without correspond-

[1] "Food Retailing Weathers Stormy Year with Best Gains in Decade," Thirty-Fourth Annual Report of The Grocery Industry, *Progressive Grocer,* April, 1967, p. 60.

ing increases in productivity. Food chain executives now realize
that these higher costs are not entirely absorbed by increased sales.

In 1948, about 1,250 supermarkets and superettes opened in
shopping centers and other locations. In 1958, the number had increased to 2,500. A considerable slowdown in new store openings
occurred in 1966, especially in relation to these earlier periods.

Store size for supermarkets has increased from an average in
1948 of 10,000 square feet to about 20,000 in 1958-1959, and remains at about this size at present.

In the 10 years from 1948 to 1958, it is estimated that 50,000
new food products sought shelf space in supermarkets and superettes.

This review is but a sweeping panorama of the dynamic developments which have taken place in slightly over a decade. It
is in light of the changing nature of retail food marketing and the
impact of these changes on retailing and the over-all economy, plus
the demonstrated interest of students and practitioners of marketing,
that this study is undertaken.

The Purposes and Scope of the Study

As the title of this study suggests, the primary objectives are
(1) identifying, (2) describing, and (3) analyzing the major forces
that have lead to the post-World War II development, growth, and
change of retail food supermarkets. The post-World War II period
has been chosen for a number of salient reasons:

1. This period has witnessed the most rapid increase in numbers
   of supermarkets as well as the most rapid increase in sales volume.
2. The supermarkets have gained their largest relative proportion
   of market share during this period.
3. This period has also witnessed, perhaps, the most dramatic
   structural changes in both economic and sociological forces, *i.e.,*
   disposable personal income, standards of living, place of residence,
   style of life, and other factors germane to a study of supermarkets.

Therefore, the time period to which this study primarily addresses
itself is 1948 through 1966. However, this study will be more than
passively interested in at least two other objectives and consequently
two additional time periods.

A brief history of the supermarketing concept as applied to

retail food marketing will be explored and analyzed in order to understand better the present operations of supermarkets. Here the concern is with the economic and social forces which resulted in the emergence of these retail institutions.

Finally, as a result of careful observation and analysis of past and present operations and developments, an additional objective of the study is to discover and analyze evolving trends which might result in specific institutional changes in the field of retail food store distribution.

Preliminary investigation leads one to believe that the major forces contributing to the development, growth, and change of retail food supermarkets in the 1948-1966 period have come from two different directions. One set of forces has emanated from sources external to the institutions themselves. These forces will be identified as external or demand forces and include such factors as population changes, income changes, changes in technology, trends toward decentralization of population, and other factors which have affected consumer incomes, tastes, and shopping habits.

In addition, certain forces have been set in motion by the retail food institutions themselves. These will be called forces emanating from the supply side, and would logically include such factors as merchandising strategies, including high volume-low margin philosophies, store location decisions, promotional strategies such as advertising, mass displays, trading stamps, and other buying and selling policies including a movement toward scrambled merchandising.

Method of Approach

The identification, description, and analysis of the major forces that have led to the post-World War II development, growth, and change of supermarkets and superettes were facilitated by examining secondary literature. Heavy emphasis was placed on such recognized official organs of the retail food field as *Super Market Merchandising, Progressive Grocer, Chain Store Age* (Grocery Executives Edition), and *Food Topics* as well as other useful periodicals. For more distant historical material, the writer utilized two well-known and authoritative publications: M. M. Zimmerman's *The Super-market: A Revolution in Distribution,* and Frank Charvat's *Super-marketing.*

In addition to the library research facilities at Indiana University and Washington State University, considerable time was spent working in the specialized library and reference materials of the Super Market Institute in Chicago, Illinois. Not to be overlooked as an excellent source of information are the many government studies and publications dealing with retail food marketing.

Considerable generalizing about future changes, developments, and emerging trends has been undertaken. These generalizations have at all times evolved as a result of a well-seasoned analysis of past and present operations and conditions.[2]

In order to establish the strengths and intensities of these evolving trends and changes and to substantiate or "fix" a pattern of these developments, supermarket leaders, trade association offi-cials, food store executives, and others possessing information per-tinent to this problem have been interviewed in depth. The approach used was that of a modified case study, and no attempt toward statistical or sampling validity was made. However, in instances where evolving trends and practices described herein are duplicated in other markets, the conclusions of this study provide a basis for policy decision of more general application for retail food super-markets and superettes.

Definition of Terms

Throughout this presentation are references to supermarkets, superettes, and other terms and institutions. For the sake of clarity, definitions of frequently used terms follow:[3]

> *Supermarket.* (a) Any food store chain or independent doing $500,-000 or more per year in sales volume. (b) The Super Market Institute defines a supermarket as "a complete departmentalized food store with a minimum sales volume of one million dollars a year and at least the grocery department fully self-service."[4]

---

[2] See Chapter 5.
[3] "Food Retailing Weathers Stormy Year with Best Sales Gains in Decade," *op. cit.,* p. 58.
[4] Super Market Institute, *The Supermarket Industry Speaks,* Eighteenth Annual Report (Chicago: Super Market Institute, 1966), p. 3.

Definition (a) will be used throughout this study. It might be noted here that prior to 1962, *Progressive Grocer* used $375,000 as its minimum volume figure for supermarkets.[5]

Superette. Any food store, chain or independent, doing from $150,-000 to $500,000 per year in sales volume. Former definition (prior to 1962)—$75,000 to $375,000 per year. Generally two types are discussed. (a) Bantam store. An all-weather store often in a crowded downtown or older neighborhood area which is frequently an attempt to salvage some existing location with little or no parking. It caters to a small area, and its customers are usually within walking distance of the store. (b) Drive-in store. Sometimes called convenience stores. Food store which has an open front and is usually a newer store out on a highway or in a suburban area. It is a convenience store for car-owning customers.

Small store. Any food store, chain or independent, doing less than $150,000 a year. Former definition—less than $75,000 a year.

Independent. An operator of 10 or less retail stores.

Chain. An operator of 11 or more retail stores.

Co-operative retailers. Retailers (generally independents) who are stockholder members of cooperative wholesale buying groups such as Certified Grocers or Associated Grocers.

Voluntary group retailers. Retailers who belong to voluntary merchandising groups sponsored by wholesalers and who operate under a common name such as I.G.A., Red and White, Spartan, Super Value, or Clover Farm.

---

[5] A really satisfactory definition of a supermarket would include features of both (a) and (b) above. The Super Market Institute definition is best from a descriptive point of view, while from another point of view the *Progressive Grocer* definition has considerable merit. Definition (a) is used throughout this study because not to do so would exclude far too many firms from the supermarket designation.

Chapter 2 | History and Discussion of Supermarket Developments

A SPATE OF articles in trade and professional journals has been written about the importance of the supermarket. In addition, several books have emerged which discuss the course and significance of the development of the supermarket institution as a major new force in the retail distribution of food products.[1]

Because of this comprehensive historical treatment by others, the major attempt here is to discuss rapidly and briefly the historical development of the supermarket and to place this development in its proper historical perspective.

This new revolution in distribution, the "Super Market," burst on the scene early in the great depression and succeeded in becoming the merchandising phenomenon of the decade despite many hazards, rebuffs, and dire predictions of nonbelievers.[2]

There seemed little question about the need for such an institution. Prior to the 1920's, the grocery business was the most backward of retailing industries. The customer was forced to buy her groceries, meats, and produce in three different locations. This was an era of product-line specialization which resulted in numerous small shops, each specializing in the sale of a specific food product. There were shops for selling meat, shops for selling baked goods and pastries, shops for dry groceries—in fact, specialized shops for selling just about any specific food commodity. This product specialization frequently meant high costs and gross inefficiencies.

---

[1] See: M. M. Zimmerman, *The Supermarket: A Revolution in Distribution* (New York: McGraw Hill Book Company, 1955), and Frank J. Charvat, *Supermarketing* (New York: The Macmillan Co., 1960).

[2] "Looking Backwards: 25 Years of Super Market Progress," *Super Market Merchandising,* August, 1955, p. 68.

These factors, in addition to the small volume of these stores, led to high retail selling prices. These conditions prevailed until the 1920's when the one-stop food market began to emerge in the form known as the combination grocery store.

Certain structural changes were developing to enhance the favorable environment and reception of the supermarket.

America was rapidly moving from the farm to the city. This movement meant a greater reliance on the retail food store by users of food products. No longer were families dependent on home-grown and home-canned foodstuffs, for as heads of households and breadwinners took up the lunch pail and moved into the factory, these families began to realize that there were economies to be attained by giving up home gardening and replacing it with retail store shopping.

With the industrialization of America also came a new-found opulence. Workers were developing new tastes, and their incomes were high. The retail stores of this period only whetted their appetites for the things to come.

America in the 1920's was also rapidly becoming a nation on wheels. The popularization of the automobile was to a large extent responsible for the development and rapid growth of the one-stop, complete food market. There was no longer any necessity to shop and purchase in the neighborhood store. The automobile made possible visits to new shopping districts, longer trips, and larger purchases.

One writer aptly characterized this whole early period of food retailing as follows:

> 100 years ago food retailing was to a considerable extent dominated by the general store. But as towns and cities grew and a greater number of food commodities came into the market, food merchants more and more specialized in the lines they sold. This, naturally, made for a large number of small specialty stores. By 1900 merchants who specialized were increasing at a rapid rate.[3]

History of Super Stores

The modern supermarket is not the first instance of a large,

---

[3] "Food Retailing—A Restless, Ever Changing Business," *Progressive Grocer*, October, 1952, p. 64.

retail food store. Goodwin describes large food markets operating under public ownership as early as 1658 in Boston.[4] Some of the early public markets were the Lexington Market of Baltimore, the Faneuil Hall Market of Boston, and the Catherine Market of New York City.[5]

These early markets were characterized as a hodge-podge of accommodations. They were housed in sheds, improvised stalls, and other makeshift facilities. Actually, these early markets were nothing more than a conglomerate of single-unit ventures. There was little over-all coordination between units; they amounted to a series of autonomous, single operations. The somewhat common characteristics of all these large public markets were that each covered a large area, that there were a large number of leased stalls, or selling booths, and that the entire operation did a significantly large volume. However, the volume of the individual stall operator was small.[6]

In addition to these public markets, there were a few private markets throughout the country which operated on basically the same principles. Notable among these were the Reading Terminal Market of Philadelphia, the Euclid and 46th Street Market of Cleveland, and the Pike Place Market of Seattle.[7]

There were other developments in food retailing which gave impetus to the evolution of the supermarket. The self-service markets in the Los Angeles area in the early 1920's, such as Ralph's and Von's, the J. B. Blood Company, and Brockelmann Brothers in Massachusetts, are examples. Certainly, the listing should also include Frank Munsey's Mohican Stores opened in 1896 and Clarence Saunders' Piggly Wiggly Stores which reportedly were the first food stores to initiate self-service. Notable also were the Alpha Beta operation opened in 1910 and converted to self-service in 1912, the Texas operations such as Weingartens, Henke and Pillot, and the ABC Stores, Inc.

---

[4] Arthur E. Goodwin, *Markets Public and Private* (Seattle, Washington: Montgomery Printing Co., 1939), p. 22.
   [5] *Ibid.,* p. 27.
   [6] Charvat, *op. cit.,* p. 12.
   [7] Zimmerman, *op. cit.,* p. 24.

Early Ingredients of the Supermarket Idea

The supermarket did not bloom as a full-grown and mature institution but evolved almost as a series of separate, distinct concepts.

To say that one element or force is the cause of a given event and that resultant consequences are effects is always difficult even in the physical sciences. This condition is certainly true in business, and, in describing "forces" or causes of given events, certain caveats are in order. However, the statement that there had to exist certain ingredients or concepts in food merchandising, as necessary or vital to the successful development of the supermarket idea, appears warranted.

One of these early concepts was cash and carry merchandising. For this idea, a great deal of credit goes to the late John Hartford of the Great Atlantic and Pacific Tea Company, who in 1912 persuaded his father to let him experiment with economy stores which rendered no delivery service and carried no credit accounts.[8]

This practice was an unusual departure from the prevailing system of the times; normally customers ran weekly and monthly grocery accounts, and even small orders were purchased personally or via telephone, and delivered by truck, wagon, or delivery boy.

Another food merchandising innovation which helped pave the way for supermarket merchandising was self-service. Self-service merchandising took its roots in southern California in 1912. A handful of merchants in this area called their particular type of self-help operation self-service.[9] Also in 1912, Clarence Saunders opened the first Piggly Wiggly Store in Memphis, Tennessee, and perhaps had more to do with the popularization of self-service than any other individual.

Self-service was regarded early as the ultimate in retail grocery store arrangement and operation. And an important lesson was soon learned by proponents and users of this new system: the American shopper is a highly impulsive creature. If she is given the opportunity to browse and look over attractive assortments,

---

[8] "Food Retailing—A Restless, Ever Changing Business," *op. cit.*, p. 33.
[9] J. S. Harrison, "Self-Service—A Development of the Machine Age," *Chain Store Age*, May, 1939, p. 39.

emotional influences frequently take over and average sales begin to go up. One early report stated that average sales per transaction went up from $.72 to $1.60, and labor costs dropped considerably after changing from clerk-help to self-service merchandising.[10]

There were indeed other factors or ingredients necessary before the supermarket idea could succeed. Manufacturers' prepackaging and canning of consistently high-quality food products was certainly important to the idea of self-service merchandising itself. The rapid increase in the number and variety of perishable foods which grocers could sell on a year-round basis forced them to enlarge their premises to provide room for coolers and refrigerated cases. The supermarket idea was about to take shape.

Early Super Store Prototypes

There appear to have been two major prototypes of the supermarket which were to emerge in the middle and later 1930's. The first of these was the so-called Los Angeles "Super," and the second was the "cheapy" supermarket which evolved in the early 1930's in the east.

The Los Angeles markets were primarily of the drive-in type— an operation which California's mild climate tended to favor. These markets were usually L or U shaped with open fronts.

These buildings were always of one story, located in outlying areas with ample adjacent parking. In many ways these drive-in markets were quite similar to the older public and private markets of the east. Each of the units of these large market stores was individually owned, but the customers looked upon the operation as a single entity.[11] One of the most elaborate of these drive-ins was the Chapman Park Drive-In Market of Los Angeles. The total investment including land and buildings was something over $400,000.[12]

Supermarkets, as distinguished from old-line large stores, did not develop in the east until the early 1930's. The depression no

---

[10] "Self-Service Layout Boosts Unit Sales from 72¢ to $1.60," *Progressive Grocer*, October, 1941, p. 20.
[11] Lucius S. Flint, "The Los Angeles Super," *Chain Store Age*, June, 1950, p. J34.
[12] "495 Autos Can Park in This New Drive-In Market," *Progressive Grocer*, October, 1929, p. 30.

doubt gave impetus to and accelerated this development. The low prices of the eastern "cheapy" made a strong bid and appeal to consumers with shrinking incomes.

In August, 1930, Michael Cullen opened his King Kullen Store in Jamaica, New York. By 1932 Cullen operated eight markets in the Jamaica area and was doing an annual sales volume of $6 million in the grocery departments alone. The keynote of Cullen's merchandising was volume, which he attempted to attain through heavy advertising of brand-name goods. The word "cheapy," which came to characterize the eastern supermarket, was indicative of both price of merchandise and surroundings. The establishments were located in abandoned factories and empty warehouses. The floors lacked coverings; partitions were torn out and counters and display fixtures were made of rough pine boards. The units thrived in low-rent locations on the fringe of thickly populated areas.[13]

Cullen's food prices were no less unusual than other facets of his operation. The following comparison of some of Cullen's prices with those of other stores will demonstrate this point:[14]

	Elsewhere	King Kullen
All 10-cent drug items	$ .10	$ .09
Campbell's tomato soup	.07	.04
U.S. rubber tires for Fords	5.50	3.78
G.E. vacuum cleaners	35.00	11.94

Here indeed was a revolution in food store distribution and pricing strategy which was worthy of the descriptive title which Cullen gave his stores: "The Price Wreckers." The supermarket was literally born with the opening of Cullen's New York operation.

Like other institutional developments, the supermarket had its adapters and modifiers, those who shape and develop the original idea to a sharp model of efficiency. One of these early shapers was Big Bear, whose spectacular merchandising tactics created a furor in the food-distribution world.[15] In December, 1932, Roy Dawson, an associate of Clarence Saunders (of Piggly Wiggly fame of Memphis, Tennessee), joined Robert Otis and opened the

---

[13] "The Cheapy Thrives," *Business Week*, February 8, 1933, p. 11.
[14] *Ibid.*
[15] "Looking Backwards: 25 Years of Super Market Progress," *op. cit.*, p. 73.

Big Bear Market in an abandoned auto factory in Elizabeth, New Jersey. The store was advertised as "the price crusher."[16] Only the first floor of the establishment which contained 50,000 square feet of space was used. Of this 50,000 square feet, 30 per cent was used for the food department.

The venture met with immediate success. Initially, the promoters had estimated sales of $1 million annually, with 50 per cent of this business from grocery sales. At the end of the first year's operation, Big Bear had taken in $3,873,000, of which 56.6 per cent represented grocery sales. The gross margin was 12.1 per cent on grocery sales, with the net profit equal to 3.6 per cent. Rental income from leased departments was 5.13 per cent of sales. The total net profit for the year's operation amounted to $166,507.[17]

The eastern supermarkets were admittedly primitive affairs, lacking the finish and polish of the California "supers." However, by prevailing standards, their prices were low and inventories enormous.

The atmosphere of the eastern supers was certainly unusual. Physical facilities frequently were crude. The advertising glittered with superlatives. But the customers came virtually in droves, and one writer described consumer reaction as follows:

> Depression weary housewives enjoyed visiting the markets, for the circusy, bizarre atmosphere that prevailed provided release for the suppressed emotions piled up within many women by the dreary monotony of depression days.[18]

By the late 1930's, the supermarket philosophy was catching on throughout America. The east had provided the basic concept, and the west gave this concept a name. The word came from Hollywood. Several prominent movie stars became interested in operating markets in California; so, naturally, this new "market" concept deserved a new and glamorous Hollywood name. The word "supermarket" came into use for describing the large, new markets. Just who specifically coined the name, and with which particular store it started, has never been established.[19]

---

[16] "Food Retailing—A Restless, Ever Changing Business," *op. cit.,* p. 64.
[17] "Looking Backwards: 25 Years of Super Market Progress," *op. cit.,* p. 74.
[18] "Food Retailing—A Restless, Ever Changing Business," *op. cit.,* p. 334.
[19] *Ibid.,* p. 332.

The Chains Fight New Competition

The chain stores were not the inventors and developers of the supermarket, but were, however, to play an important role in shaping the future of this concept.[20] The chains had developed a system of so-called economy stores. These stores were quite similar to the small, independent combination grocery store of the 1920-1930 period. The feature which made these operations quite distinct from their independent counterparts was, of course, chain ownership, which meant standardization of much of their operation, centralized policy making, somewhat better physical facilities as a result of better financing, and stronger capital positions.

Prior to the introduction of the supermarket by independent operators, the chains had usually been able to undersell the independent grocery. The chain stores had what was characterized at this time as "high buying skill and low buying prices." This attribute was their competitive forte. There was no Robinson-Patnam Act until 1936. And prior to the passing of this legislation, the chains were notorious for extracting large quantity discounts, advertising allowances, dummy brokerage fees, and other concessions from sellers.

The independents had a difficult time competing with these economy-store operations of the chains. The economy stores were clerk-service establishments, sometimes offering free delivery and credit. The cost structure of the supermarket made competition too difficult, if not outright impossible, for chain economy stores. The chains were also to be criticized from several social and economic sources.[21] This was the period of the "inquisition of the chains."

By 1929, the average chain food store was doing an annual sales volume of $46,000, compared with the sales of $17,380 which the independents chalked up annually. The rapid expansion and growth of the chains during the 1920's created deep resentments and antagonisms on the part of many people.[22]

---

[20] U.S. Circuit Court of Appeals, 7th District, testimony by Malcolm P. McNair, "United States vs. the Great Atlantic and Pacific Tea Company," Docket 9221, *Records and Briefs,* Vol. II, p. 194.

[21] See: Godfrey M. Lebhor, *Chain Stores in America* (New York: Chain Store Publishing Co., 1959).

[22] "Looking Backwards: 25 Years of Super Market Progress," *op. cit.,* p. 70.

Lebhor lists several of the charges quoted against the chains:[23]
1. Chains took money out of community
2. Drove local retailers out of business
3. Chains tended to depersonalize the community
4. Destroyed opportunities for young men
5. Charged chains were producing a nation of clerks
6. Paid lower wages than other employers
7. Did not bear their full share of local taxes
8. Practiced unfair methods of competition
9. Tended toward monopoly
10. Raised the over-all cost of marketing

That the chain food stores ever posed an actual threat to the independent food store operator is somewhat doubtful. A brief glance at Figure 2.1 should help explain why.

In 1929, before the widespread introduction of the supermarket concept, chains accounted for 17 per cent of the total number of retail food stores. By 1935, however, the proportion of chains had decreased to 13 per cent of the total.

In terms of percentage of dollar food sales, the chains were making a more significant showing.

In 1933, the time of the emergence of the early supermarkets, the chains were accounting for 16 per cent of the total number of retail food stores and were doing 44 per cent of the total retail food store volume. By 1939, however, after the supermarket idea had become accepted, the chains accounted for only 10 per cent of the total number of stores and their percentage of total volume had fallen from 44 per cent to 36.6 per cent.

The chain operators were frightened and began to fight back against this new merchandising innovation which was upsetting all standards for food store operations and efficiency. The chains rapidly came to realize that, in order to survive, they too must adopt and utilize supermarket tactics. And they did (see Figure 2.2). For example, a young chain of neighborhood stores known as the Union Premier Stores of Philadelphia (now Food Fair) operated some 26 neighborhood stores of the conventional clerk-service type, with annual sales of $1,626,329. In 1933, the management decided after a survey of "super" operations to convert to this new type of operation. All stores of this firm were closed between

---

[23] Lebhor, *op. cit.,* pp. 148-157.

Figure 2.1.   Chain grocery stores as a percentage of total grocery stores.

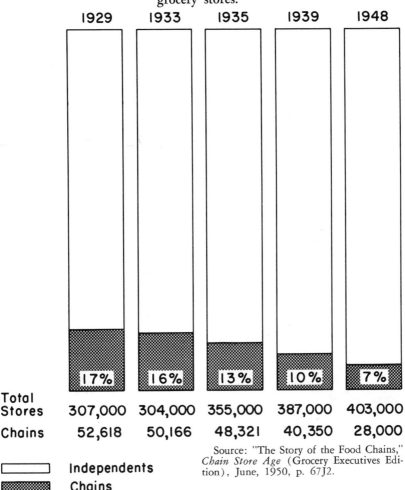

	1929	1933	1935	1939	1948
	17%	16%	13%	10%	7%
Total Stores	307,000	304,000	355,000	387,000	403,000
Chains	52,618	50,166	48,321	40,350	28,000

☐ **Independents**

▓ **Chains**

Source: "The Story of the Food Chains," *Chain Store Age* (Grocery Executives Edition), June, 1950, p. 67J2.

1933 and 1937 and replaced with 22 supermarkets featuring self-service, cash-and-carry merchandise, and lower retail prices. The new supers did an annual volume of $13,760,000, or $600,000 per unit compared with $62,000 per unit for the neighborhood store.

Between the years 1934-1937, A & P closed 933 of its 4,306 units in 38 cities, replacing them with 204 supermarkets. A look at Table 2.1 shows that this closing of a large number of smaller units and replacement with fewer, large supers was unquestionably

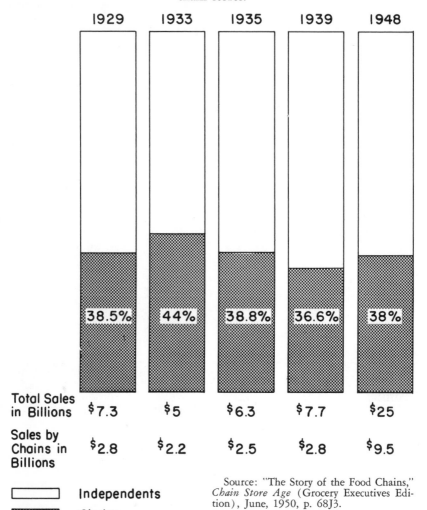

Figure 2.2. Percentage of total retail grocery sales accounted for by chain stores.

	1929	1933	1935	1939	1948
	38.5%	44%	38.8%	36.6%	38%
Total Sales in Billions	$7.3	$5	$6.3	$7.7	$25
Sales by Chains in Billions	$2.8	$2.2	$2.5	$2.8	$9.5

☐ Independents

▓ Chains

Source: "The Story of the Food Chains," *Chain Store Age* (Grocery Executives Edition), June, 1950, p. 68J3.

the vogue of the times. This movement was to be the keystone of the chains' fight for survival. In this same period, Kroger dropped 355 stores and added 33 supers. Safeway dropped 272 stores and added 28. The chains were convinced that they must replace inefficient neighborhood units in super-invaded areas with super-type markets of their own.

One study compared the operation of an average A & P neighborhood store (clerk-services) and an average A & P super. The super did $13,741 per week as opposed to the neighborhood unit's $943. The super's sales expenses were about 12.5 per cent of sales as opposed to 20 per cent for the neighborhood unit. The smaller store secured a higher percentage of its sales from the comparatively profitless staples, while the supermarket sold a greater percentage of the higher-profit items.[24] On the basis of these observations, there appeared little doubt of the supermarket's ability to sell more goods at a lower price, thus creating a greater profit potential.

TABLE 2.1

STORES AND SALES OF LEADING FOOD CHAINS
(sales in millions of dollars)

Chain	1925		1929		1939		1949	
	Stores	*Sales*	*Stores*	*Sales*	*Stores*	*Sales*	*Stores*	*Sales*
A & P	14,034	$440	15,418	$1,054	9,260	$976	4,600	$2,837
Safeway	1,050	39	2,660	210	2,859	386	2,177	1,193
Kroger	2,559	116	5,494	287	3,958	243	2,204	807
American	1,792	109	2,730	143	2,272	115	1,671	409
First National	1,731	49	2,002	76	2,244	124	1,083	354
National Tea	761	47	1,627	90	1,073	57	655	274
Colonial	480	14	811	32	552	46	374	169

Source: "The Story of The Food Chains," *Chain Store Age* (Grocery Executives Edition), June, 1950, p. 70J5.

The period of the late 1930's was one of rapid growth and expansion of the supermarket idea. The supermarket was soon to become the major institution for distributing food products at retail to a hungry America.

The Structure of the Retail Food Industry

To the uninitiated, the retail food industry generally appears as a hodge-podge of institutions employing a number of organizational, ownership, and operational arrangements. In reality, although a degree of complexity does prevail in the structure of the retail food store industry, this structure can be classified into a number

[24] "Looking Backwards: 25 Years of Super Market Progress," *op. cit.*, p. 76.

of categories which generally simplify the analysis and arrangements of types of stores, ownership, and kinds of stores.

This structure is not really a mirrored reflection of reality, but is simply a set of verbalized models used for purposes of description, classification, and analysis. These "ideal constructs" conform to reality, but there naturally occurs some duplication and overlapping of institutional arrangements.

Retail food stores can logically be classified into three groups: (1) size and type, (2) ownership, and (3) kinds of food stores.

Number and Sales of Grocery Stores by Size of Establishment

Retail food stores have been categorized as falling into three size classifications:[25]

1. Supermarkets or large stores
2. Superettes or middle-sized stores
3. Small stores

The supermarket was defined earlier in Chapter 1 as any store, chain or independent, doing $500,000 sales volume or more per year. The Super Market Institute defines a supermarket for membership purposes as a complete, departmentalized food store having self-service in grocery sales and a minimum volume requirement of one million dollars per year.

The first definition and the volume requirement of $500,000 appear most useful for the study. The annual surveys of *Progressive Grocer,* which use this volume requirement, are perhaps the most complete and authoritative in the field.

One must remember that in this discussion of supermarkets a particular type of retail food store with somewhat unique characteristics is being discussed. The exact volume requirement is something of an academic point.

The distinction between a supermarket and a superette is merely one of degree and not wholly one of kind. Arbitrarily, and solely for the purpose of ease of classification, assume that the superette is a medium-sized store having an annual volume between $150,000

---

[25] The basis for this discussion of the structure of the retail food store industry was taken from "Food Retailing—A Restless, Ever Changing Business," *op. cit.,* p. 6. The figures for the various operations and general industry results are from "Food Retailing Weathers Stormy Year with Best Sales Gains in Decade." Thirty-Fourth Annual Report of the Grocery Industry, *Progressive Grocer,* April, 1967, p. 60.

and $500,000. Superettes are operated in the main much like their larger counterparts, the supermarkets, with departmentalized organization and self-service operation.

The small store is indeed a mixture of characteristics and is hard to categorize on the basis of operational features. The small store is frequently a neighborhood food store, operating on either the basis of clerk-help, such as the vanishing "mom and pop" stores, or on the basis of self-service. The one characteristic that is essential to the classification of a small store is low volume. The small store must be doing under $150,000 per year to meet the requirements of this classification. Figure 2.3 clarifies these definitional descriptions.

Note from Figure 2.3 that, while supermarkets account for only 14.4 per cent of the total number of stores, they account for 71.3 per cent of the total dollar sales volume of retail grocery stores. Another interesting observation is that superettes, with 12.7 per cent of the total number of stores, account for nearly the same percentage of dollar sales volume. Of the total number of retail grocery stores, 72.9 per cent are classed as small stores. Yet these small stores have only 15.9 per cent of total sales volume.

Number of Stores and Sales by Kinds of Ownership

Figure 2.3 shows retail food stores, including supermarkets, superettes, and small stores, as either independents or chain organizations.[26]

An independent operation may therefore consist of supermarkets, superettes, and small stores. A chain organization may follow the same pattern. In other words, the chain units may be supermarkets, superettes, or small stores, or some combination of each.

In 1966, there were slightly more chain supermarkets than independents, considerably more independent superettes than chains, and a far larger number of independent small stores than chain small stores. A glance at Figure 2.3 shows that, in terms of sales volume, the independents outrank the chains in store sales except for supermarkets; in this area the difference is not large, $22.5 billion for independents, compared with $27.9 billion for chains.

---

[26] See the definitions in Chapter 1.

Figure 2.3. U.S. grocery sales and number of retail grocery stores by type of store, 1966.

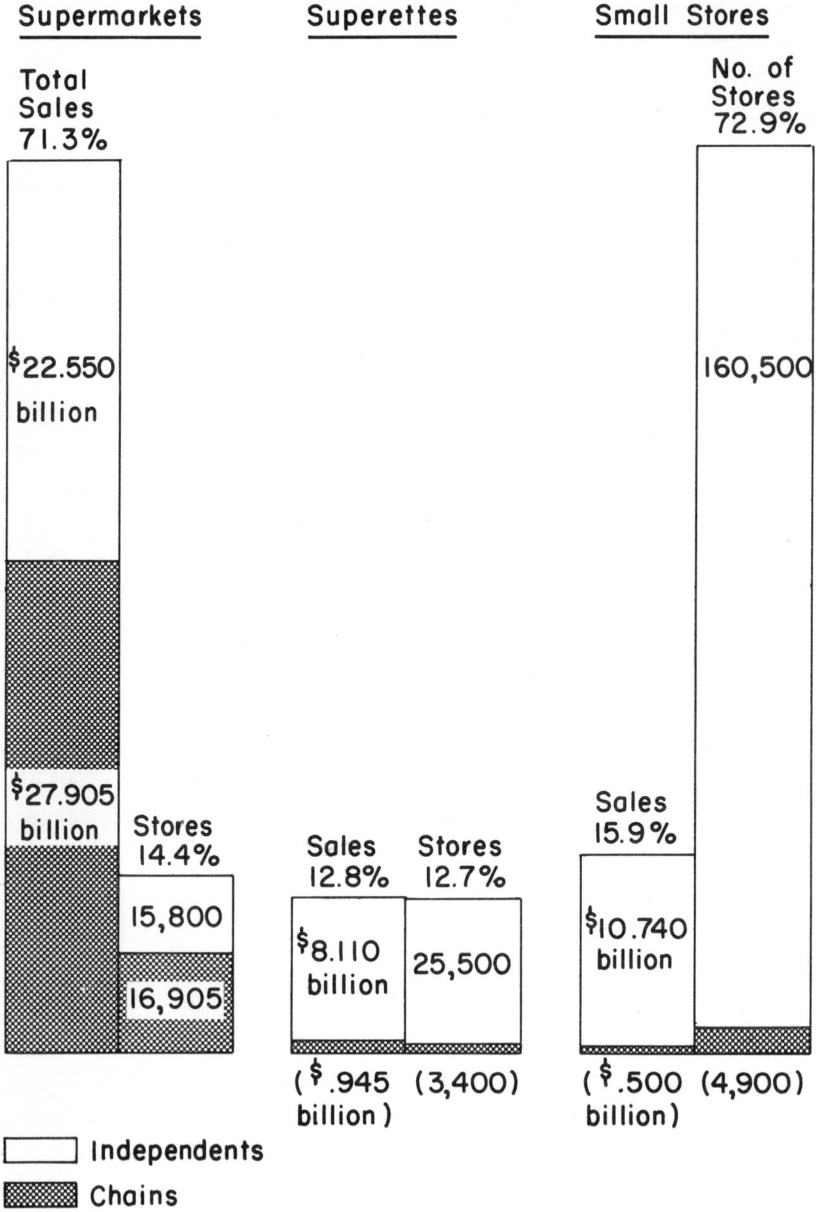

Supermarkets　　Superettes　　Small Stores

Total
Sales
71.3%

No. of
Stores
72.9%

$22.550
billion

160,500

$27.905
billion

Stores
14.4%

Sales
15.9%

Sales
12.8%

Stores
12.7%

15,800

$10.740
billion

16,905

$8.110
billion

25,500

($.945
billion)

(3,400)

($.500
billion)

(4,900)

☐ Independents

▨ Chains

Source: "Food Retailing Weathers Stormy Year with Best Sales Gains in Decade," Part I, Thirty-Fourth Annual Report, *Progressive Grocer,* April, 1967, p. 67.

The independent retail food store appears to be holding its own in nearly all categories.

Retail Food Stores Classified as to Kind

Table 2.2 will help to explain this classification. The names of the different kinds of food stores are more or less self-explanatory. The grocery and combination stores are by far the most important for observation and analysis. As a matter of fact, this category accounts for nearly 85 per cent of total retail food store volume. This fact is perhaps not so surprising when one recalls that supermarkets, both chain and independents, which fill the bulk of the combination store category, do 71.3 per cent of the total retail food store volume.

The Significance of the Supermarket and Superette in 1966

Table 2.3 summarizes Figure 2.3 by bringing together the number of stores and sales volume of each according to the kind of ownership arrangement, *i.e.,* independent or chain.

TABLE 2.2

NUMBER OF RETAIL FOOD STORES BY KIND FOR 1966

Grocery and Combination Stores
    Independents, including delicatessens
        (one to 10 units) 201,800
    Chains (11 or more units) 27,205

Total Grocery and Combination Stores 229,005

Specialty Food Stores (chain and independent)
    Meat and fish markets 20,500
    Bakery products stores 18,600
    Fruit and vegetable markets 9,100
    Candy, nut, and confectionery stores 15,300
    Other food stores 10,000

Total Specialty Stores 73,500

Total Retail Food Stores 302,505

Source: "Food Retailing Weathers Stormy Year with Best Sales Gains in Decade," Part I, Thirty-Fourth Annual Report, *Progressive Grocer,* April, 1967, p. 66.

In 1966, total retail grocery store sales were $70.75 billion. Of this total, supermarkets were responsible for $50.45 billion, or 71.3 per cent of total sales, and the superettes for $9.055 billion, or 12.8 per cent of total sales. On the basis of these facts alone, there can remain little doubt as to the relative importance of these two major institutions of food retailing. One study reported that, of the 20 largest retail institutions, 10 were food retailing chains primarily operating supermarkets.[27]

TABLE 2.3

GROCERY STORE SALES AND NUMBER OF STORES BY SUPERMARKETS, SUPERETTES, AND SMALL STORES BY KIND OF OWNERSHIP

Type of Organization	Number of Stores	Store Sales (billions of dollars)	Per Cent of Sales
Supermarkets			
Independents	15,800	$22.550	31.9
Chains	16,905	27.905	39.4
Total	32,705	$50.455	71.3
Superettes			
Independents	25,500	$ 8.110	11.5
Chains	3,400	.945	1.3
Total	28,900	$ 9.055	12.8
Small Stores			
Independents	160,500	$10.740	15.2
Chains	4,900	.500	0.7
Total	165,400	$11.240	15.9
Total	227,005	$70.750	100.0

Source: "Food Retailing Weathers Stormy Year with Best Sales Gains in Decade," Part I, Thirty-Fourth Annual Report, *Progressive Grocer*, April, 1967, p. 63.

Table 2.4 dramatically shows a strong relationship between larger weekly sales per square foot of selling area and larger areas of selling space. Many operators are discovering real economies of scale by moving to larger-sized supermarket operations. In 1948,

[27] *The Fortune Directory of the 500 Largest U.S. Industrial Corporations*, Editors of Fortune, *Fortune*, July 15, 1966, p. 256.

the average size of the new supermarkets opened was 10,000 square feet of selling area. This size increased to nearly 20,000 square feet of selling area in the 1959-1960 period and has remained at about that same level to the present time.

In 1966, 2,890 new supermarkets were opened, and the ratio of new stores (supermarkets) to existing supermarkets was approximately 1 to 11.

TABLE 2.4

SALES PER SQUARE FOOT BY SIZE OF SUPERMARKETS[a]

Sales Range	Average Square Feet Sales Area	1966 Average Sales	Weekly Sales per Square Foot
$ 500,000-$ 750,000	5,477	$ 592,000	$2.08
750,000- 1,000,000	6,863	878,000	2.46
1,000,000- 2,000,000	9,150	1,318,000	2.77
2,000,000 and over	15,056	2,999,000	3.83

[a] Average square foot of selling area was computed as follows: 1966 sales ÷52=weekly sales. Weekly sales÷weekly sales per square foot=average square feet of selling area.

Source: "Food Retailing Weathers Stormy Year with Best Sales Gains in Decade," Part I, Thirty-Fourth Annual Report, *Progressive Grocer*, April, 1967, pp. 80-81.

Superettes present some interesting statistics pertaining to their operation. Tables 2.4 and 2.5 point up comparisons between the operations of supermarkets and of superettes.[28]

As was mentioned earlier, little practical difference except size exists between a supermarket and a superette. Both are self-service operations, generally cash and carry, and have lower prices than the small, clerk-help, neighborhood store. The independents seem to dominate the superette field, while the chains appear to dominate the supermarkets.[29] This situation is largely accounted for by the much greater ease of entry into the superette field by independents, because of simpler financing and lower capital requirements.

[28] A complete discussion of the superette is beyond the scope of this presentation. Therefore our concern from this juncture will be more involved with the larger and more important of these institutions, the supermarket.

[29] For a more comprehensive discussion of superettes, see Rom J. Markin, "The Superette: Opportunity for the Independent Owner," *Journal of Retailing*, Spring, 1963, p. 18.

TABLE 2.5

SALES PER SQUARE FOOT BY SIZE OF SUPERETTES[a]

Sales Range	Average Square Feet Sales Area	1966 Average Sales	Weekly Sales per Square Foot
$150,000-$200,000	3,084	$170,000	$1.06
200,000- 250,000	3,317	219,000	1.27
250,000- 300,000	3,740	280,000	1.44
300,000- 375,000	4,117	334,000	1.56
375,000- 500,000	4,477	433,000	1.86

[a] Average square feet of selling area was computed in the same manner as for Table 2.4.

Source: "Food Retailing Weathers Stormy Year with Best Sales Gains in Decade," Part I, Thirty-Fourth Annual Report, *Progressive Grocer,* April, 1967, pp. 80-81.

Integration As a Means of Growth

Much of the nation's retail food business is done by supermarket organizations, and many of these supermarkets are large-scale retail organizations doing an annual volume of over $1,000,000. The more recent rapid growth of supermarkets can be attributed primarily to three factors: (1) increased sales of supermarkets, (2) new stores opened by both chains and independents, and (3) stores acquired from other companies by both chains and independents. The chain stores have, however, far outdistanced the independents in terms of growth via acquisitions.

The purpose of this section is to analyze more closely the role of the chain organizations in retail food store distribution and to look at such factors as the proportion of food sales accounted for by chains, as opposed to independents.

The Role of the Chain in Retail Food Sales

Progressive Grocer estimated that retail food store sales in 1966 amounted to $70.750 billion. Of this amount, 71.3 per cent was attributed to supermarkets and 39.4 per cent to chain-operated supermarkets.[30]

[30] "Food Retailing Weathers Stormy Year with Best Sales Gains in Decade," Part I, Thirty-Fourth Annual Report, *Progressive Grocer,* April, 1967, p. 63.

TABLE 2.6

OWNERSHIP OF SUPERMARKETS BY TYPE OF ORGANIZATION:
CHAINS VS. INDEPENDENTS

Type of Organization	Number of Supermarkets	Per Cent of Total Supermarkets	Sales (billions of dollars)	Per Cent of Total Supermarket Sales
Chain	16,905	51.6	$27.905	55.3
Independent	15,800	48.4	22.550	44.7
Totals	32,705	100.0	$50.455	100.0

Source: "Food Retailing Weathers Stormy Year with Best Sales Gains in Decade," Part I, Thirty-Fourth Annual Report, *Progressive Grocer*, April, 1967, p. 63.

By successfully emulating and adapting the supermarket practices of the early independents, the chains soon became the nation's major distributors of retail foodstuffs. Table 2.6 reports the relative position of chain and independent-ownership-controlled supermarkets. The table shows that in 1966, of the total supermarkets numbering 32,705, no less than 16,905 of these stores were operated by chain organizations (operating 11 or more stores). This amounted to 51.6 per cent of the total supermarkets and accounted for 55.3 per cent of total supermarket sales.

Integration

When an organization of retail stores or one retail store acquires a unit of the same type from another company or individual, then the firm is said to have grown through integration of existing establishments. Integration can take several forms. The two most prevalent types are horizontal (the example just presented) and vertical. Vertical integration occurs when a retailer acquires wholesaling or manufacturing facilities.

Integration of both types has played a major role in the growth and development of large supermarket organizations, especially those owned by chains. Many chain and independent supermarkets have integrated to some extent vertically, and, in the case of several chain supermarkets, vertical integration including manufacturing has been very substantial. The remarks here will be limited to a discussion of horizontal integration and its effect on supermarket size and growth. The most extensive analysis of growth through merger and acquisition is perhaps that done by the Federal Trade Commission in its study, *Economic Inquiry into Food Marketing*. Highlights of this investigation are reported herein.[31]

Table 2.7 shows that the acquisition of food stores by corporate chains operating 11 or more stores has increased sharply in the postwar period, with the year 1955 marking a substantial increase. From 1949 through 1954, the annual averages were: 9 acquiring chains, 11 acquisitions, 93 stores, and $52.6 million current sales; from 1955 through 1958 there were 22 chains, 63 acquisitions, 420 stores, and $401 million sales.

Not all corporate food chains have been active in the merger movement via acquisition. A few of the large chains were especially active in making food store acquisitions in the years studied by the Federal Trade Commission (1949 to 1958). The 10 chains which acquired the largest number of stores and the largest volume of retail sales are shown in Table 2.8. Only one of these 10 companies acquired food stores in 1949, 1950, or 1952. Two to five made acquisitions in 1951, 1953, and 1954. In 1955, seven made acquisitions, followed by nine in 1956, five in 1957, and nine in 1958.

The 1958 sales of food stores acquired by the 10 chains over the entire period amounted to $996 million, or 61 per cent of the $1,639 million in sales of all stores acquired by corporate chains. The $996 million was 11.9 per cent of the 1958 sales of the 10 chains.

The immediate question becomes, "Why all the merger activity?" What are the forces and factors behind this merger movement? Several reasons for this have been advanced.[32]

1. The nature and spirit of the supermarket industry has been one of growth and change. Managers are willing to experiment with new methods and are anxious to see store operations and size increase.
2. Profits, as witnessed in the previous section, have been good and reasonably steady. The seeming invulnerability of the food

[31] U.S. Federal Trade Commission, *Economic Inquiry into Food Marketing,* Part I (Washington: U.S. Government Printing Office, 1960), pp. 127-156.
[32] See Charvat, *op. cit.,* pp. 182-183.

TABLE 2.7

FOOD STORE ACQUISITIONS BY FOOD CHAINS, BY YEARS,
1949 TO 1958

Year of Acquisition	Acquiring Companies	Acquisi- tions	Stores Acquired	Annual Sales When Acquired
1949	6	6	72	$ 66,180
1950	5	5	5	3,889
1951	10	12	69	27,829
1952	5	10	273	70,800
1953	11	12	71	86,617
1954	17	20	70	60,580
1955	23	48	455	434,166
1956	36	70	439	397,325
1957	34	54	363	322,520
1958	38	78	421	450,003
Total	83[a]	315	2,238	$1,919,909

[a] Column does not add, as some companies made acquisitions in more than one year.

Source: U.S. Federal Trade Commission, *Economic Inquiry into Food Marketing*, Part I (Washington: U.S. Government Printing Office, 1960), p. 128.

TABLE 2.8

FOOD STORE ACQUISITIONS BY 10 LARGE FOOD CHAINS: 1949 TO 1958

Company	Acquisitions	Stores Acquired	Annual Sales When Acquired
American Stores Company	5	93	$ 34,443
Colonial Stores, Inc.	10	99	121,906
Food Fair Stores, Inc.	6	67	107,731
The Grand Union Co.	15	128	128,417
Jewel Tea Co., Inc.	2	43	56,234
The Kroger Co.	5	130	174,064
Lucky Stores, Inc.	4	56	72,612
National Tea Co.	24	485	251,612
Safeway Stores, Inc.	25	67	33,016
Winn-Dixie Stores, Inc.	11	306	221,070
Total 10 Chains	107	1,474	$1,201,105

Source: U.S. Federal Trade Commission, *Economic Inquiry into Food Marketing*, Part I (Washington: U.S. Government Printing Office, 1960), p. 138.

industry to economic recession builds in a somewhat safe growth factor. New merchandising activities for earnings are constantly being sought.

3. Larger concerns have more and more begun to realize the economies of scale which come from increased size. Operators are able to spread costs and risks over a larger number of operations.

4. It is becoming increasingly more difficult to find satisfactory locations. As new locations become more dear, firms are seeking to get new outlets via merger or acquisition.

5. The larger firms are stronger in terms of the marketable securities they have to exchange for the shares of the smaller companies than are the firms under $100 million annual volume. This gives the larger firms an advantage in acquisition through stock exchange.

6. The smaller organizations were started and have been operated by owner-managers. As these men have become older and faced the need of retirement, finding new personnel to act as managers has posed a serious threat. Facing this situation many of the operators simply sold out to larger chains.

7. Finding suitable and available sources of outside capital has also been a serious problem impeding expansion by smaller-sized organizations. Failing to obtain borrowed or debt capital and lacking the means or facilities to sell equities, the smaller concerns could expand only through retained earnings. Frequently, the threat of stronger competition, and the inadequacy of the smaller concerns to grow, forced them or resigned them to sell out.

One of the more important problems facing the economy today is the increase in concentration that has developed by way of mergers and acquisitions. Section 7 of the Clayton Act, as amended in 1950, seeks to deal with this type of concentration and has become a major instrument of antitrust policy. The statute broadly encompasses those situations whereby one corporation engaged in commerce obtains the stock or assets of another corporation engaged in commerce. The language of the statute is not complex, but its application in a given situation is often difficult because it creates as a standard of illegality the tendency of a merger to "substantially lessen competition" or "create a monopoly." The result has been that legal and economic yardsticks for mergers have developed slowly as the agencies and courts have sought to apply these general standards to concrete situations.

Both the Federal Trade Commission and the Department of Justice are authorized to enforce Section 7. Insofar as the food industry is concerned, the Federal Trade Commission has been by far the more active. Between 1950 and 1965, it instituted 17 food industry proceedings, while four were brought by the Department of Justice.[33]

In the retail sector, the Federal Trade Commission initiated four proceedings involving acquisitions. Two of these, one involving Consolidated Foods Corporation, the other Grand Union Company, were disposed of by consent settlements calling for divestiture and a limited ban on the acquisition of other retail outlets for a specified number of years. In a recent proceeding against the National Tea Company, the Commission found a substantial lessening of competition and prohibited further acquisitions for a period of 10 years. The fourth proceeding against the Kroger Company is as yet not finalized. The one Department of Justice case in the retail sector involved a local acquisition in the Los Angeles market. This case was lost by the Government in the trial court, but on appeal to the Supreme Court, the trial court was reversed and divestiture was ordered.[34]

The Supreme Court's ruling in this particular situation has handed federal antitrusters a weapon which should sharply curtail merger activities among larger food retailers. In this decision, the court ruled illegal the acquisition of Shopping Bag Stores, the sixth largest grocery chain in Los Angeles, by Von's Grocery Company, the third largest. The acquisition, had it been approved, would have made Von's the second largest chain in the area.

In what appears to be a historic decision, the court firmly stated that mergers of substantial, healthy competitors must be blocked in markets that, while highly competitive, are nevertheless tending toward oligopoly.[35] Previous court decisions had dealt mainly with more concentrated markets. The high court's reasoning was that in the Los Angeles area there existed a threatening trend of lessening competition in which the grocery business was being concentrated into the hands of fewer and fewer owners. In the 10 years before

---

[33] "Food from Farmer to Consumer," *Report of the National Commission on Food Marketing* (Washington: U.S. Government Printing Office, June, 1966), p. 84.

[34] *Ibid.*, p. 84.

[35] For a fuller account of this decision and its likely effect on future merger activities in food retailing, see "High Court Bars Merger of Rivals," *Business Week,* June 4, 1966, p. 36.

the merger took place in 1960, the number of single-store owners declined from 5,365 to 3,818. During roughly the same period, chain stores grew from 96 to 150. The court's opposition to the merger was not abated by the fact that the combined food chains controlled only a relatively small portion (7.5%) of the city's $2.5 billion retail market, that many independent food stores remained, or that competition after the merger continued to be vigorous.

There is little doubt that this decision will arm both the Federal Trade Commission and the Department of Justice with a more powerful antimerger weapon and that growth via merger and acquisition will become exceedingly more difficult. It would appear from the widely hailed but largely anemic "Report of The National Commission on Food Marketing" that concentration of food retailers into larger and larger economic units is likely to be subject to increasing criticism and control.[36]

Thus, the larger supermarkets, especially those operated by corporate chains, through aggressive merchandising strategies, sound financial backing, and a strong willingness and desire to grow, have come to command a significant role in retail food distribution.

The independents have not "withered on the vine," however. Much of the nation's retail food store needs continue to be supplied by the independent merchant. The independents have not taken an indifferent and apathetic view of the corporate chains' growth. They have fought back, in many instances with vigor and determination. A discussion of their efforts at fighting back is examined in the subsequent section.

Growth of Voluntary and Cooperative Organizations

The large chain supermarkets have gained some competitive edge over the independent markets with economies effected through buying techniques. The independent retail food merchants, especially those with supermarket and superette units, realized that in order to remain competitive they, too, must obtain buying economies.

Two rather unique methods to accomplish this aim were hit

---

[36] "Food Report Feeds Controversy," *Business Week,* May 28, 1966, pp. 173-174.

upon by the independent food retailers and also by the wholesalers who serviced them. The wholesalers realized that the passing of the independents would in turn mean losses of great amounts of volume and possibly the extinction of many of the wholesalers themselves.[37]

The first of these two methods involved cooperation among the independent retailers. The retailers decided to operate their own wholesale houses. In cooperative association, the retailers mail in their orders, thus eliminating the need and expense of a wholesale salesman. The wholesale aspect is concerned with operating the warehouse and delivering groceries on a regular schedule. The retailer provides the money to finance the wholesale house and either pays cash for the groceries or receives a week's or 10 days' credit. Most of the wholesale (cooperative) houses operate on very low expenses. The simple average operating expense ratio of four such wholesalers was 4.4 per cent.[38]

A large share of the profit is returned to member stores as patronage dividends, and only a small proportion is carried to surplus. The expense percentage represents the margin charged the retailers. The earlier houses developed mainly by handling groceries. Many today, however, have taken on fuller lines, including frozen foods, drugs, toiletries, and produce. The retailer-owned wholesalers often have limited lines of goods under their own brands.

Trends in Retailer-Owned Cooperative Food Wholesalers

Table 2.9 shows the number of retailer-owned cooperatives reporting in the survey of the Federal Trade Commission in 1959. This total represents nearly a complete census of these organizations.[39] As can be seen from this table, the number of retailer-owned cooperatives has grown significantly in the 1948 to 1958 period, and the number of retail stores serviced by this method has grown even more rapidly.

[37] Paul D. Converse, "Twenty-five Years of Wholesaling—A Revolution in Food Wholesaling," *Journal of Marketing*, Vol. XXII, No. 1, July, 1957, p. 40.
[38] *Ibid.*, p. 47.
[39] U.S. Federal Trade Commission, *op. cit.*, p. 159. The Federal Trade Commission sent questionnaires to 182 firms. One was unincorporated, 16 proved not to be cooperatives, and 19 had moved without leaving forwarding addresses or had gone out of business.

Other interesting highlights from the Federal Trade Commission study of the retailer-owned cooperatives will now be reviewed.[40] Total wholesale sales of the reporting cooperatives amounted to $544 million in 1948 and $2,031 million in 1958. Cooperative wholesalers owned by retail stores do 97 per cent of their business with members; this contrasts sharply with the voluntary associations, which do a significant volume with nonmembers. Between 1948 and 1958, their aggregate sales increased nearly 10 times as much as those of all other general-line wholesalers. Estimated retail sales of member stores of all cooperatives in the continental United States increased from about $2.4-$2.7 billion in 1948 to $7.6 billion in 1958.[41] By 1966, this figure had roughly reached about 14 billion dollars.[42] The retailer-owned cooperative has been a significant factor in the strengthening of the independents' competitive position.

Perhaps the single weakest factor in the cooperative wholesale ventures is the lack of stability which results from a rapid turnover of members. Less than half the members in the Federal Trade Commission 1958 study had belonged to the same cooperative as long as five years. In spite of this weakness, however, the retailer-owned cooperatives have met in large part the objectives of their origination and use—they have enabled the independent merchant to combat the chains' tactics by supplying his merchandise requirements at a greatly reduced cost.

The second movement to combat the advantages of the large chain food stores took the form of so-called voluntary wholesale organizations. This movement has, by far, the larger growth and importance. One count showed 456 voluntary wholesalers with 59,000 affiliated retailers.[43] These associations are called voluntaries because they voluntarily associate with the wholesaler. The wholesaler secures a group of retailers who agree to buy all or nearly all of their merchandise from him. The wholesaler, in turn, must furnish the retailers with merchandising assistance in operating their stores and give them a franchise to use the sponsor's name on their

---

[40] *Ibid.*, pp. 157-169.
[41] *Ibid.*, p. 175.
[42] Exact figures are unavailable from industry sources. The author's estimate is an approximation based upon growth in the cooperatives' market share and total food store sales.
[43] U.S. Federal Trade Commission, *op. cit.*, p. 47.

TABLE 2.9
MEMBERSHIP OF RETAILER-OWNED COOPERATIVES OPERATING IN 1958, BY DECADE OF ORGANIZATION: 1943 AND 1958

Decade	Companies Organized		1948	Members 1958	1958 Cumulative	Stores Served (member and non-member 1958)
	Number	Cumulative				
1881-1890	1	1	2,072	1,723	1,723	1,723
1891-1900	1	2	1,063	1,091	2,814	1,091
1901-1910	1	3	130	300	3,114	304
1911-1920	12	15	5,889	5,556	8,670	5,661
1921-1930	26	41	6,383	8,000	16,670	9,348
1931-1940	38	79	4,465	5,376	22,046	5,632
1941-1950	44	123	4,325	7,823	29,869	7,980
1951-1958	13	136		1,273	31,142	1,364
Year not Reported	10	146	809	1,033	32,175	1,180
Total	146	146	25,136	32,175	32,175	34,283

Source: U.S. Federal Trade Commission, *Economic Inquiry into Food Marketing*, Part I (Washington: U.S. Government Printing Office, 1960), p. 159.

stores. The most prominent of these voluntary groups are IGA, Red and White, and Clover Farm.

Because the retailers voluntarily submit their business to the wholesaler, the wholesaler is not faced with the necessity of providing salesmen. The wholesaler receives the orders from the affiliated retail stores, accompanied by signed blank checks for payment. The wholesaler's facilities, of late, have become the epitome of modern efficient operation. His buildings are one story on an assembly-line or conveyor-belt basis. He employs modern techniques of palletization and fork-lift trucks. On occasion, the wholesaler employs merchandising men to help the retailers in such everyday problems as store operation and design and layout of facilities. Accountants are employed to aid the retailer in setting up records and to make out income tax statements.

Trends in Wholesaler-Sponsored Voluntary Retail Groups

The 330 wholesalers which responded to the Federal Trade Commission study are said to represent nearly the complete national totals of this type of store operated in 1958. The highlights of this study are now summarized.[44] One third of these started their groups after 1953, almost two thirds after 1943, and 99 per cent after 1923. The sponsored stores, 35,822 in 1958, were 14 or 15 per cent of all grocery stores, as compared with 8 or 9 per cent for sponsored stores in 1930.

All but 88 of the 330 reporting wholesalers had 100 or fewer stores in their sponsored groups, but the average number of stores was 109—as compared with 138 in 1929. Nearly 3 per cent of the stores in 1958 were reporting sales over $1 million per year; 11 to 12 per cent between $375,000 and $1 million; and 85 to 86 per cent less than $375,000 (see Table 2.10).

The 1958 sales were estimated by the Federal Trade Commission to be $9 billion. By 1966, this figure had roughly reached about $21.0 billion, or about 28 per cent of national grocery store sales.[45]

---

[44] *Ibid.* For a more comprehensive look at the results of this study, see pages 204-234.

[45] Exact figures are unavailable from industry sources. The author's estimate is an approximation based upon growth in the cooperatives' market share and total food store sales.

TABLE 2.10

NUMBER OF SPONSORED AND OTHER STORES SERVED BY SPONSOR-WHOLESALERS, AND AVERAGE SIZE OF VOLUNTARY GROUPS, BY GEOGRAPHIC DIVISIONS: 1958

Geographic Division	Sponsor-Wholesalers	Stores Served			Sponsored Stores as a Per Cent of Total	Average Number of Sponsored Stores per Voluntary Group
		Sponsored Stores	Other	Total		
New England (Maine, N.H., Vt., Mass., R.I., and Conn.)	39	3,172	9,563	12,735	24.9%	81.3
Middle Atlantic (N.Y., N.J., and Pa.)	64	8,045	13,568	21,613	37.2	125.7
East North Central (Ohio, Ind., Ill., Mich., and Wis.)	80	8,720	24,999	33,719	25.9	109.0
West North Central (Minn., Iowa, Mo., N. Dak., S. Dak., Nebr., and Kans.)	37	5,781	8,020	13,801	41.9	156.2
South Atlantic (Del., Md., D.C., Va., W. Va., N.C., S.C., Ga., and Fla.)	43	1,461	21,751	23,212	6.3	34.7
East South Central (Ky., Tenn., Ala., and Miss.)	21	1,908	10,599	12,507	15.3	90.9
West South Central (Ark., La., Okla., and Tex.)	25	2,277	11,807	14,084	16.2	91.1
Mountain (Mont., Idaho, Wyo., Colo., N. Mex., Ariz., Nev., and Utah)	8	411	9,051	9,462	4.3	51.4
Pacific (Wash., Ore., and Calif.)	13	4,047	16,526	20,573	19.7	311.3
Total	330	35,822	125,884	161,706	22.2%	108.6

Source: U.S. Federal Trade Commission, *Economic Inquiry into Food Marketing*, Part I (Washington: U.S. Government Printing Office, 1960), p. 206.

The basic philosophy of both the retailer-owned cooperative and the wholesaler-sponsored voluntary group is to make retailers better merchants. Their goal is one of operating good retail stores and selling at prices as low as the chains. That they have been successful is indicated by the fact that the independents in recent years have been holding their share of the market reasonably well. The voluntary and cooperative wholesale organizations have been faced with the problem of supplying their customers with needed services and at the same time holding down their expenses to a ratio comparable to other competitive types of wholesalers. As can be witnessed from Table 2.11, some success has been attained in this area.[46]

One can observe from Table 2.11 the rather slow growth in the expense ratios of merchant wholesalers and the reverse trend, *i.e.,* a rather slow decline in the expense ratios of voluntary group wholesalers. Observe also that retail cooperative group wholesalers are still below the voluntary group wholesalers in their operating expense ratios, but the gap does appear to be narrowing.

Summary

Before the advent of the supermarket, the primary food stores were the "economy units" of the chains. These stores, although far superior to earlier institutions engaged in food marketing, were in many respects inferior to the supermarket. The supermarket evolved because a need existed for a lower cost method of distributing food products.

Prior to the 1920's, grocery retailing was something of a backward industry. This was an era of product-line specialization which afforded little or no economies of scale for food marketing. As a result, margins were relatively high. Several other factors tended to favor the growth and development of a new food marketing innovation such as the supermarket. The movement of large numbers of people from farm to city meant a greater reliance on the retail store by users of farm products. The rise in the ownership

---

[46] See Kendall A. Adams, "Achieving Market Organization through Voluntary and Cooperative Groups," *Journal of Retailing,* Summer, 1966, pp. 19-28.

TABLE 2.11

AVERAGE GROCERY WHOLESALING OPERATING EXPENSES AS A PER CENT OF SALES FOR SELECT YEARS

Type of Wholesaler	1939 (per cent)	1948 (per cent)	1954 (per cent)	1958 (per cent)	1963 (per cent)
Merchant Wholesalers	9.2	12.5	13.1	14.4	14.6
Cash and Carry Wholesalers	4.9	4.9	5.0	10.9	n.a.[a]
Wagon Distributors	9.4	14.5	14.0	14.7	13.0
Voluntary Group Wholesalers	10.6	8.3	7.4	n.a.[a]	6.2
Cooperative Group Wholesalers	5.0	4.6	4.4	n.a.[a]	4.5

[a] These figures were not shown in the source.

Source: U.S. Bureau of the Census, *Census of Business* (Washington: U.S. Government Printing Office), for the respective years.

and usage of the automobile gave consumers new mobility to seek out stores with lower prices and wider selections.

The supermarket had several forerunners; the large public and private city markets stimulated the development of the supermarket. The basic ingredients of supermarketing, cash-and-carry merchandising, and self-service, evolved after King Kullen's experiment in Jamaica, Long Island, and the California store openings in the early 1930's. The supermarket idea was quick to catch on, and other independents rapidly followed the examples set by these earlier successes. The chains also began to adapt many of their stores to self-service and cash-and-carry bases. During this period, literally thousands of the smaller chain units were closed and replaced by the newer supermarkets.

The large corporate chain supermarkets now control a significant share of the food and grocery market. These chains have grown by building more units and by acquiring other stores via merger and acquisition. The chains have been eager to adopt the supermarket concept, and, consequently, many of the smaller chain grocery stores have been closed and replaced by the larger supermarket type of establishment. The independent grocery retailer appears to be fairly well holding his own, however, in terms of over-all market share. Many independents have bolstered their competitive position by forming voluntary and cooperative groups. The formation of these hybrid chains has enabled the independents to gain buying economies and acquire merchandising assistance, thus permitting them to compete more effectively.

The food retailing industry is actually dominated by the corporate chains and the affiliated independents whose methods of operation and merchandising strategies are much like those of the chains. Both the chains and the affiliated independents have increased their market shares at the expense of the unaffiliated retailers. But for several years now the unaffiliated independents' share of the market has been stabilizing at about 10 per cent. From here on, it would appear that if either the chains or affiliated independents are to keep up their growth pace, the gains of one will, of necessity, have to come from the other and not from small local grocers.

An interesting question is: "Which of the two groups, chains or affiliated independents, is better prepared for the impending struggle?" The affiliated groups would appear to enjoy a major advantage in management ownership. A man running an affiliated supermarket, which he owns, is working for himself; his chain store counterpart is merely an employee supervising his company's investment, not his own.

However, some chain organizations are reacting by increasing the managerial autonomy of their store managers, allowing them to do the buying, hiring, pricing, and merchandising. In short, the manager runs the store much as if he owns it.

Chapter 3	Environmental Forces Favoring the Growth and Development of Supermarkets

THIS CHAPTER deals with the environmental forces and factors which have fostered the growth and development of supermarkets and superettes, or what might be called large self-service, cash-and-carry food stores.

All business firms operate within a business environment, and supermarketing institutions are no exception. The state of activity within this competitive, or business, environment can and does greatly affect the state of "health" of the business institutions. Thus, the saying, a "rising tide lifts all ships," is appropriate at this juncture because it describes aptly the relationship which exists between the institution and the environmental factors which bear on its success or failure. Given favorable environmental factors such as increasing population, favorable movements in population, rising incomes, and others, the business institution is more likely to grow, prosper, and expand. Of course, the opposite can happen if environmental factors are not favorable.

In many ways, the analysis and discussion of this chapter conform closely to what Howard calls the uncontrollable dimensions of marketing.[1] These dimensions are composed of the social, political, and economic environment of the company.

An Analysis of Demographic Forces Favoring Growth and Development of Supermarkets

The demographic forces at work today in the economy of the United States are viewed by many businessmen as the panacea of

---

[1] John Howard, *Marketing Management Analysis and Decision* (Homewood, Illinois: Richard D. Irwin, Inc., 1963), p. 5.

present and future business ills. Indeed, the rather remarkable changes which have taken place in the postwar era in terms of over-all changes in population growth, size and composition of families, and trends toward population decentralization have fostered a favorable climate for many business institutions, especially those dealing with consumer durable and nondurable goods. These changes benefited the supermarket and superette by permitting the institutions to sell more goods and to take on additional food and nonfood lines demanded by new and emerging age and living groups.

The Growth in Population

The population of the United States is one of two key elements which stimulate the tone and vigor of the American market. The other, of course, is income, which will be discussed subsequently.

In 1900, 39.7 per cent of the United States population lived in urban places (more than 2,500 inhabitants) as opposed to the remaining 60.3 per cent who lived in rural environments (places of less than 2,500 inhabitants). By 1960, these percentage relationships had reversed themselves, resulting in 69.8 per cent living in urban places as opposed to 30.1 per cent living in rural areas.[2]

Much of this change resulted from the migration of people from farm to urban or suburban living arrangements. In 1960, only about 9 per cent of the total number of families actually lived on farms; nearly 70 per cent of the total population resided in cities of more than 2,500 people, while the remainder lived in rural nonfarm communities.[3]

When large numbers of people left farming for urban residences, the result, of course, was a greater reliance on retail grocery stores for food needs. The urban population constitutes the dominant market for consumer goods, including such items as food and nonfood lines sold by supermarkets.

Between 1790 and 1950, the population of the United States doubled five times. Before World War II, it was generally conceded by most so-called prognosticators that the maximum population of the United States would be about 165 million people. How-

[2] U.S. Bureau of the Census, *1960 Census of Population,* Vol. I, *Characteristics of the Population,* Part A, Number of Inhabitants (Washington: U.S. Government Printing Office, 1961), p. xii.
[3] *Ibid.*

ever, as a result of postwar marriages and the baby boom, the United States passed the 165 million mark by 1955, and by 1966 was a nation of slightly less than 200 million people. This increase in total population has called forth a corresponding increase in demand for goods and services. Food and general merchandise products carried by supermarkets and superette stores have, also, naturally been favored by increased sales warranted by the new impetus on demand.

One writer, in analyzing the increase in population and its corresponding effect on demand, states that, by using longer-run trends in spending per capita for selected outlay categories, this difference in numbers has amounted to an increment in demand for output of at least $15-$20 billion annually between 1947 and 1957, in constant 1957 dollars.[4] These estimates would cover not only consumption expenditures but also residential nonfarm consumption, and school construction. Undoubtedly, the effect on food store sales caused by changing population forces has been significant.

In many ways, the interest in population changes is even more heightened when the changes in households are analyzed rather than just number of persons. For marketing purposes, the change in number of households (households include both families and individuals living alone) and the rate of household formations are of extreme importance. Certainly the household remains the primary buying unit for many commodities, including both food and general merchandise items.

The number of United States households has grown more rapidly than total population. During the first half of this century, for example, while the population doubled, the number of households almost tripled. In the decade since the close of the war, households have increased by 11 million units, more than twice as many as were ever previously added in a single decade.[5] Between 1966 and 1975, the number of households in the United States is likely to increase by 11 million to a total of 69 million.[6]

---

[4] George J. Stolnitz, "Our Growing Population: Threat or Boon," *Business Horizons*, Vol. 2, No. 2, Summer, 1959, p. 43.
[5] Phillip M. Hauser, "The Challenge of Tomorrow's Markets," *Journal of Marketing*, Vol. 24, No. 1, July, 1959, p. 2.
[6] *Ibid.*, p. 2.

The primary difference between the rate of growth of households and of total population is accounted for by the decrease in the size of households. At the first census, there were some 5.8 persons per household; by 1966, there were only 3.30 persons per household. And if current low birth rates continue, some slight decrease in persons per household is likely to be evidenced by 1975.

The character of United States households is very likely to change significantly throughout the coming years. During the late 1950's a high proportion of households were headed by women or men in their so-called "middle years"; over 57 per cent of the household heads during this period were between 25 and 54. During the present decade (1965-1975), this proportion will be reduced appreciably, for about three quarters of the increase in households will be accounted for by those whose heads are at the younger and older ends of the age continuum.

One type of household which grew rapidly during the 1955-1965 period, but which will likely remain at about the same size during 1965-1975, is that category of households headed by men or women living alone. The growth of this household category generally called forth an acceleration of activities on the part of supermarkets to meet the demands of these buyers—demands which were focused on such items as frozen foods, ready-mix preparations, health and beauty aids—especially dietary foods, vitamins, and other drug items—and fast-preparation items.

The real thrust which threatens to swell the number of households in the U.S. will come in the category "husband-wife" households. This category will increase about 8,000,000 to 49,600,000 in 1975 (in the previous decade it was up only 5,300,000).[7] The young married couples who will largely constitute this category are also likely to have somewhat specialized requirements for food and groceries.

Some other demographic forces which foster growth and development of business institutions, such as supermarkets, can be seen by looking at Figure 3.1. Here it can be seen that youngsters, teen-

---

[7] Laurence A. Mayer, "Why the U.S. Population Isn't Exploding," *Fortune,* April, 1967, p. 192.

Figure 3.1.   Domestic population trends by age groups, total
United States.

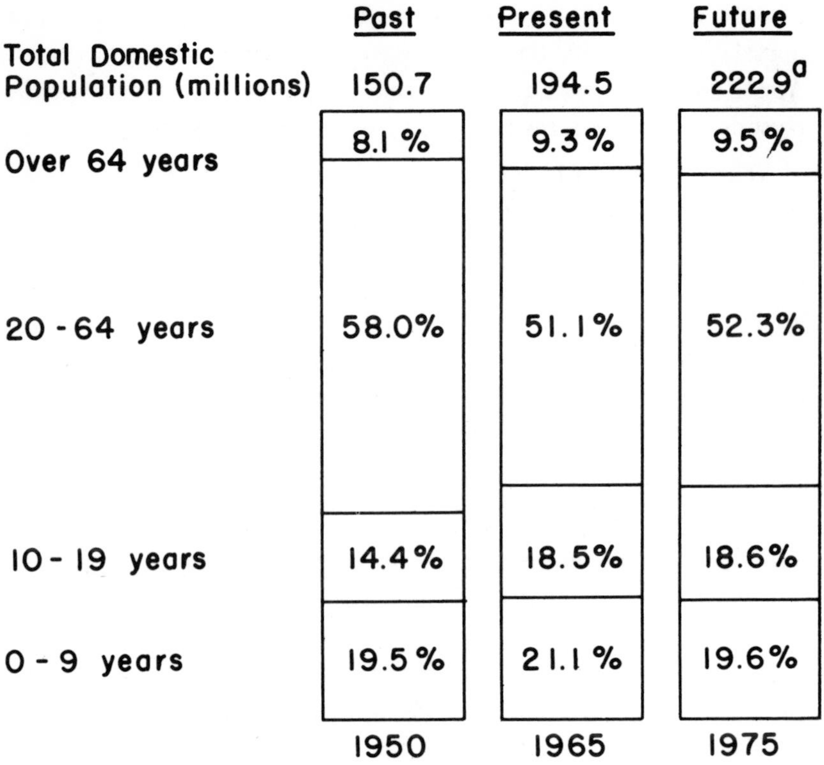

	Past	Present	Future
Total Domestic Population (millions)	150.7	194.5	222.9[a]
Over 64 years	8.1 %	9.3%	9.5%
20 - 64 years	58.0%	51.1%	52.3%
10 - 19 years	14.4%	18.5%	18.6%
0 - 9 years	19.5%	21.1 %	19.6%
	1950	1965	1975

[a] Based on Series B predictions.
Source: Department of Commerce, Bureau of the Census, *Current Population
Reports,* Series P-25, No. 329.

agers, and oldsters will continue to increase their shares of the total,
while the middle-age group (20-64 years) will diminish propor-
tionately. Many firms are already beginning to recognize the potential of catering to one specific age group by modifying facilities,
offering extra services, and expanding product lines.

Some companies have found the senior-citizen market a readily
available and fertile field. A whole new class of product offerings,
generally listed as geriatrics, has recently become available to be
merchandized to this group. This product line includes general
medicinal tonics, dietary supplements, digestive aids, cathartics, di-
uretics, oral and external analgesics and anti-rheumatics, and prod-

ucts for denture wearers.[8]

These products, as well as other drug and toiletry items, lend themselves well to supermarket merchandising and may very well partially account for the large success of general merchandise lines by supermarkets and superettes.

The 10- to 19-year-old group increased its numbers rapidly in the postwar era, and expectations are for slight continued growth in the future. The number of children between 15 and 19 will increase by almost 95 per cent between 1950 and 1975.

The magnitude of spending by teenagers is largely a matter of conjecture, with estimates for the most part running around $10 billion per year.[9] Much of this spending can be labeled discretionary, however, and is almost principally confined to nondurable goods. The teenage spender has often been associated with low-cost items such as soft drinks, phonograph records, home permanents, magazines, and lesser accessories. Some retail stores, however, are experimenting with "teen centers" in which the young customers are exposed to a wider range of temptations.[10] Food marketers would be well apprised to watch the spending movements and behavior of this young, yet affluent, group.

The Race for the Suburbs

Several causes have been noted as affecting the movements to, and development of, the suburban areas. By 1912, the expansion of electric street railways made possible in many communities for at least the higher-paid workers to escape from the gloom and shadow of the factory walls and the confinements of the dirty inner city. The movement by the labor unions for shorter working days and better pay and the success of many of these efforts gave the laboring class reduced work schedules and more discretionary time.

The real impetus to this movement and race to the suburbs was the growing popularity of the automobile and the improvements in roads and highways. Industries, too, began to seek plant and factory

---

[8] David E. Wallin, "A Marketing Profile of the Senior Citizen Group," *Marketing's Role in Scientific Management* (Chicago: American Marketing Association, 1957), p. 259.

[9] *Markets of the Sixties,* by the Editors of *Fortune* (New York: Harper and Brothers, 1958), p. 14.

[10] Paul E. Smith, "Merchandising for the Teen Age Market," *Journal of Retailing,* Summer, 1961, pp. 9-14.

locations out of conventional city locations, for they realized that workers could easily follow them via auto, streetcar, and bus and, also, that suppliers could continue to fill their needs via spur railroad lines and now, of course, motorized freight.

The changing structure of metropolitan and suburban areas brought important changes in retail food store distribution just as the over-all increase in population was accompanied by a rising retail food store volume. The following tables may help in part to show these changes.

TABLE 3.1

SHIFT IN POPULATION IN 140 CENTRAL CITIES OF THE UNITED STATES WITH 50,000 POPULATION AND OVER, FOR THE YEARS 1930 AND 1940 (in thousands)

	1930 Population	1940 Population	Per Cent Increase 1940 over 1930
Central Cities	40,343	42,796	6.1
Outside Central City Area[a]	17,259	20,109	16.9

[a] By census definition the area "outside the central city" is immediately adjacent to the city.

Source: U.S. Bureau of the Census, *Sixteenth Census of the U.S., 1940 Population*, Vol. 1 (Washington: U.S. Government Printing Office, 1942), p. 61.

Table 3.1 shows data on 140 central cities which in 1940 had 50,000 population or more. Note that the percentage increase of 1940 over 1930 for population within the central city was 6.1 per cent. But the percentage increase of 1940 over 1930 for the area outside the central city was 16.9 per cent. Between 1940 and 1950, these movements outside the central city were even more pronounced. The percentage increase 1950 over 1940 for the central city was 13.9, and the percentage increase of 1950 over 1940 for the area outside the central city was 35.5. As shown in Table 3.3, from 1960 to 1965, movements of population to areas outside the central city continued, at about the same average annual rate as during the 1940 to 1950 period.

TABLE 3.2

SHIFT IN POPULATION IN 168 CENTRAL CITIES OF THE UNITED STATES WITH 50,000 POPULATION AND OVER, FOR THE YEARS 1940 AND 1950 (in thousands)

	1940 Population	1950 Population	Per Cent Increase 1950 over 1940
Central Cities	43,391	49,412	13.9
Outside Central City Area[a]	25,887	35,087	35.5

[a] By census definition the area "outside the central city" is immediately adjacent to the city.

Source: U.S. Bureau of the Census, *Number of Inhabitants, U.S. Summary Census of Population* (Washington: U.S. Government Printing Office, 1950), pp. 1-69.

TABLE 3.3

SHIFT IN POPULATION IN 212 CENTRAL CITIES OF THE UNITED STATES WITH 50,000 POPULATION AND OVER, FOR THE YEARS 1960 AND 1965 (in thousands)

	1960[a] Population	1965 Population	Per Cent Increase 1965 over 1960
Central Cities	57,790	59,612	3.2
Outside Central City Area[b]	54,533	64,201	17.7

[a] For comparability with data from the Current Population Survey, figures from the 1960 census have been adjusted to exclude members of the Armed Forces living in barracks and similar types of quarters.
[b] By census definition the area "outside the central city" is immediately adjacent to the city.

Source: U.S. Department of Commerce, Bureau of the Census, *Current Population Reports*, Series P-20, No. 151.

The movement to the suburbs has had many implications and ramifications for retail food supermarkets. The suburban market was not just a group of city dwellers transplanted to the sylvan countryside, but, rather, a whole new breed of opulent, well-informed buyers who were demanding new products, new services, and new facilities to fulfill their wants. The socio-economic status of these buyers differed markedly from other groups. One source reporting about the new suburban market made the following observations:[11]

[11] "The Lush New Suburban Market," *Fortune*, Vol. XLVIII, No. 5, November, 1953, p. 131.

1. The median family income in 1950 for the suburban area is $5,100 as against $3,600 for the city.
2. 75 per cent of the suburban families owned their homes as compared with 41 per cent for the city.
3. Approximately 27 per cent of the residents in the suburbs were under 14 years of age. In the city itself this age group accounted for only a little more than 21 per cent.

As Americans moved to the suburbs, retail food supermarkets moved with them by locating in new shopping centers, along new highways and adjacent to new suburban developments.[12] These stores sold the bulk of the staple food needs to the new suburban dwellers and experimented with gourmet foods, new beverages, and a whole host of general merchandise lines including barbecue sets and rotisseries, outdoor cooking supplies of all sorts, household supplies including shovels, rakes, hoes, and planters.

An Analysis of Economic Forces Favoring Growth and Development of Supermarkets

The economic changes witnessed by the United States economy during the last few decades have been phenomenal. The changes wrought, in turn, on the marketing scene have been no less amazing. The United States consumer is at an all-time high in terms of purchasing power and want-satisfying ability.

Figure 3.2 is illustrative of the growth and dynamism of the over-all economy and shows that gross national product has grown steadily during the 1950's and 1960's. Directly allied with this increase in over-all economic activity is consumer buying power, which also has grown quite remarkably. Table 3.4 is a partial explanation of this growth in the consumer's ability to purchase goods.

From 1948 to 1966, disposable personal income has increased from $189.3 billion to $505.3 billion, or 167 per cent. Personal consumption expenditures have increased from $178.3 billion in 1948 to $464.9 billion in 1966, or 161 per cent. Expenditures for food products, excluding alcoholic beverages, have increased during this same period from $48.2 billion to $90.7 billion, or an increase of 88 per cent. Expenditures for food products as a percentage of

---

[12] The movement of retail food stores to outlying areas will be discussed more fully in the next chapter.

Figure 3.2.   Trend of total business activity, Gross National Product (GNP). Seasonally adjusted annual rates.

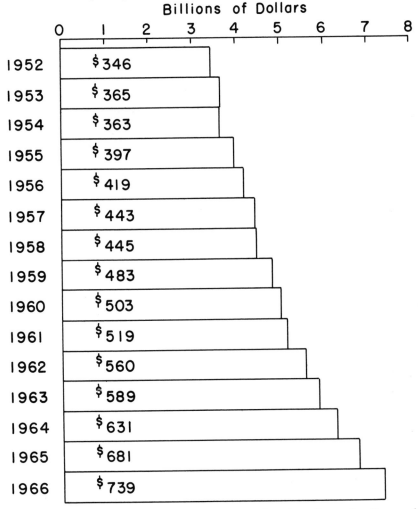

Billions of Dollars

	0	1	2	3	4	5	6	7	8

1952	$346
1953	$365
1954	$363
1955	$397
1956	$419
1957	$443
1958	$445
1959	$483
1960	$503
1961	$519
1962	$560
1963	$589
1964	$631
1965	$681
1966	$739

Source: U.S. Department of Commerce, Office of Business Economics, *Survey of Current Business* (Washington, D.C.: U.S. Government Printing Office, July, 1962, September, 1965, and May, 1967).

personal consumption expenditures have declined from 27 per cent in 1948 to 19.5 per cent in 1966.

The American consumer's ability to increase his expenditures for food when faced with rising incomes is handicapped of course by the size limitations of the human stomach. Given this situation,

TABLE 3.4

DISPOSABLE PERSONAL INCOME, PERSONAL CONSUMPTION EXPENDITURES,
EXPENDITURES FOR FOOD EXCLUDING ALCOHOLIC BEVERAGES
FOR 1948-1966
(seasonally adjusted annual rates)

Year	D.P.I.[a] (billions of dollars)	P.C.E.[b] (billions of dollars)	F.E.[c] (billions of dollars)	F.E./P.C.E.[d] (per cent)
1948	$189.3	$178.3	$48.2	27.0
1949	189.7	181.2	46.4	25.6
1950	207.7	195.0	47.4	24.3
1951	227.5	209.8	53.4	25.4
1952	238.7	219.8	55.8	25.3
1953	252.5	232.6	56.6	24.3
1954	256.9	238.0	57.7	24.2
1955	274.4	256.9	59.2	23.0
1956	292.9	269.9	62.2	23.0
1957	308.8	285.2	65.2	22.8
1958	317.9	293.5	67.4	22.9
1959	337.3	313.8	68.1	21.7
1960	354.2	328.2	70.0	21.3
1961	363.6	338.0	71.0	21.0
1962	384.4	355.4	74.4	20.9
1963	402.6	373.8	76.5	20.4
1964	436.6	401.4	79.9	19.9
1965	469.1	431.5	85.2	19.7
1966	505.3	464.9	90.7	19.5

[a] Disposable Personal Income.
[b] Personal Consumption Expenditures.
[c] Food Expenditures excluding alcoholic beverages.
[d] Food Expenditures divided by Personal Consumption Expenditures.

Sources: U.S. Department of Commerce, *U.S. Income and Output* (Washington: U.S. Government Printing Office, November, 1958), p. 152, and U.S. Department of Commerce, *Survey of Current Business* (Washington: U.S. Government Printing Office, July, 1962; May, 1967; and January, 1964).

expenditures for food as a percentage of personal consumption expenditures are quite likely to decline. Only a constant stream of new and better products can hope to hold up this relationship. Perhaps this fact is a partial explanation for the increased emphasis on nonfoods in supermarkets.

The Changing Distribution of Incomes

In addition to the quantitative changes in disposable personal income and personal consumption expenditures in the United States, another far-reaching and significant change has taken place in the distribution of income shares. Simon Kuznets has made an important contribution in the study of upper income shares.[13]

In the first three decades of this century, the United States began to develop its first so-called mass market. In 1900, almost half the family units in the United States had less than $2,000 of income in 1959 prices. During the 1920's, the most significant market development was the creation of a sizable "lower-middle" income class based on family units in the $2,000-$4,000 income class. By 1954, over 40 per cent of all family units had an after-tax income between $4,000 and $7,500, and their income was about 40 per cent of the total.[14]

Currently, about 16 per cent of all families in which the head is under 35 have earnings of over $10,000 per year. But by 1975 that percentage will have increased to an estimated 35 per cent. In absolute numbers we now have roughly 2 million families in the indicated age-earning bracket; 10 years hence, there will be over three times as many.

A number of factors will contribute to this development. First of all, young families will become about half again as numerous as they are now. And second is the configuration of the prevailing income distribution curve. Today, relatively many young families are clustered in the $7,000-$10,000 income category. Given the over-all improvement in earnings expected in the course of the next 10 years, many families will be found in the upper-income brackets. In summary, the general improvement in economic fortunes expected for the years ahead, in conjunction with population growth, will make for a pronounced increase in the number of young upper-income families. By 1975, young and affluent homes—where the head is under 35 and incomes exceed $10,000—will account for

---

[13] Simon Kuznets, *Shares of Upper Income Groups in Income and Savings* (New York: National Bureau of Economic Research, Inc., 1953).

[14] *Markets of the Sixties, op. cit.,* pp. 91-92.

an estimated 15 per cent of total buying power.[15] (All figures are based on present-day dollars.)

Thus, this group will constitute a significant and rapidly growing market segment, and for the food stores catering to the needs and the fancies of the young and well heeled, the prospects are imposing.

Changes in Expenditures in Food Stores

The statistics of Table 3.4 show that food expenditures, excluding alcoholic beverages, have increased from $48.2 billion in 1948 to $91 billion in 1966, or 88 per cent. The point to be made here is that much of this gain is going to supermarkets and superettes or those stores generally known as "grocery stores" or "combination markets." The supermarkets have accommodated themselves to changes in consumer food tastes and also to the technological changes in food as a product. But even more important, these institutions have spearheaded a revolution in food retailing services. The many environmental forces at work certainly appear to have been conducive to the growth, development, and perpetuation of the retail food supermarket.

An Analysis of Technological Forces Favoring Growth and Development of Supermarkets

The technological developments which originally fostered the growth and development of supermarkets during the early 1930's remain today essentially the major technological forces which continue to foster growth and expansion of supermarkets.

As originally conceived by many of its promoters, the early supermarket could not have come about without the development of two highly important technological achievements—the automobile and refrigeration.

The automobile was necessary to get the customers to the markets and home again with their weekly food supplies. Without this new mobility, American food shoppers might still be trekking to the corner grocery for the day's food requirements.

---

[15] Fabian Linden, "Family Formation," *The Conference Board Record,* The National Industrial Conference Board, Inc., Vol. IV, No. 2, February, 1967, pp. 38-40.

In two respects, refrigeration has played an equally important role for the development of supermarkets. First, home refrigerators enabled the consumer to make once-a-week shopping trips for meats, vegetables, and other perishables. And, second, without in-store refrigerators such as dairy and meat cases, produce cases, and beverage coolers, supermarkets would have been greatly restricted in the types as well as number of items they could have carried.

Even today, the automobile and new methods and techniques of refrigeration continue to play a highly significant role in the continued development and expansion of supermarkets and superettes.

The Automobile

Automobile ownership, as witnessed by registrations and shown in Table 3.5, has increased from 27,372,397 units in 1940 to 81,-050,000 units in 1966. This figure represents something like a 200 per cent increase in a 27-year period.

The automobile is the number-one method of travel in the United States today. American consumers spend 11 times as much on buying and operating cars as they do on all forms of public transportation, local and long distance—buses, planes, subways, taxis, and trains.[16]

During 1966, Americans spent an estimated $30 billion on cars —nearly $16 billion for gasoline and oil. The automobile industry sold 9,300,000 new cars in 1965, and given a reasonably prosperous economy, estimates are that new car sales in 1975 will approach 11,500,000 units.[17] There is a basic and prosaic explanation for the widespread success of the automobile in the United States: more and more Americans can and want to move about, and, increasingly, the automobile is the most convenient way of doing so. Surely, the automobile will continue as an important element for the successful growth and development of supermarkets and superette food stores.

---

[16] U.S. Department of Commerce, *Survey of Current Business,* October, 1965, p. 28.

[17] Jeremy Main, "A Slow Getaway for the Auto Market," *Fortune,* June 1, 1967, pp. 112-115.

TABLE 3.5

PASSENGER CAR REGISTRATIONS AND FACTORY DOLLAR SALES
OF PASSENGER CARS IN THE UNITED STATES
FOR THE YEARS 1940-1966

Year	Registrations (000)	Factory Sales (000,000)
1940	27,372	$ 2,371
1945	25,691	57
1950	40,185	8,468
1955	51,951	12,453
1956	54,003	9,755
1957	55,692	11,198
1958	56,644	8,010
1959	59,316	10,530
1960	61,432	12,164
1961	63,261	10,319
1962	66,111	13,072
1963	69,059	14,427
1964	71,984	14,837
1965	75,252	18,400
1966	81,050	17,033

Sources: Registrations—U.S. Department of Commerce, Bureau of Public Roads, Annual Report, *Highway Statistics,* for years shown; Factory Sales—Automobile Manufacturers Association, Detroit, Michigan, *Automobile Facts and Figures.*

The Importance of Refrigeration

Just a few short years ago, home refrigeration by electrical means was considered a luxury of the rich. Manufacturers reported sales of electrical refrigerators in 1926 of 205,000 units. However, by 1966, this number had increased to 4,916,000 (see Table 3.6).

Perhaps no other appliance has so changed the food, eating, and shopping habits of the American consumer as has the mechanical refrigerator. This appliance permitted the consumer to shop less frequently, by enabling her to purchase and store items that once had to be immediately consumed.

The principle of refrigeration, including the deep-freeze concept, greatly altered and expanded the food lines which could successfully be merchandised by supermarkets via self-service techniques; fresh meats, cold cuts, produce, frozen foods, cheese, dairy products, and a host of other items were successfully handled without undue concern for spoilage and deterioration.

The home freezer and the freezer case of the supermarket have made possible the rapid expansion of frozen food lines. Frozen foods, which now include complete dinners, attained an estimated retail volume of $3.50 billion in 1966.[18]

TABLE 3.6

Manufacturer's Sales of Refrigerators and Home Freezers by Number of Units for the Years 1946-1966

Year	Refrigerators	Home Freezers
1946	2,100,000	210,300
1947	3,400,000	607,000
1948	4,766,000	690,000
1949	4,450,000	485,000
1950	6,020,000	884,000
1951	3,731,000	1,032,500
1952	3,196,000	1,118,200
1953	3,287,000	1,049,800
1954	3,135,000	943,000
1955	3,820,000	1,045,000
1956	3,382,000	919,000
1957	3,350,000	925,000
1958	3,116,700	1,100,900
1959	3,785,000	1,205,400
1960	3,475,000	1,045,000
1961	3,480,000	1,050,000
1962	3,775,000	1,070,000
1963	4,125,000	1,090,000
1964	4,545,000	1,110,000
1965	4,930,000	1,160,000
1966	4,916,000	1,096,000

Source: *Merchandising Week,* January issue, 1947-1967.

Other Technological Developments

Many technological developments have had the direct result of changing techniques for commercial processing and preparing food products and for indirectly changing the buying and shopping habits of the consumer. The usual result has been to favor the growth and development of supermarket stores by attracting more customers, increasing unit sales by stimulating impulse buying, and

[18] Dollar volume for retail sales of frozen foods for 1966 is unavailable. This figure represents the author's own projection based upon past trends and recent sales increases.

taking on new food and nonfood lines and thus broadening the merchandising base.

Techniques of canning and freezing were not generally satisfactory during the 1920's. However, the later perfection of these food-processing techniques has generally resulted in stimulating sales in all major food categories. For instance:

1. Annual consumption of commercially canned fruit increased from 12.1 lbs. per capita in the 1925-1929 period to 23.6 lbs. in 1965; canned citrus juice consumption from .05 lbs. per capita in 1929 to 4.02 lbs. in 1965.[19]

2. Much the same trend is true of vegetables. In the average year of the 1925-1929 period, per capita consumption was 150.4 lbs., of which 104.9 lbs. were fresh and 45.5 lbs. were processed. In 1965, per capita consumption of vegetables increased to 208.4 lbs.—100.4 lbs. fresh and 108.0 lbs. processed.[20]

3. Frozen fruits and juices were purchased at the rate of only 0.34 lbs. per capita annually in 1925-1929; by 1965, per capita consumption was 8.50 lbs. Frozen vegetable consumption averaged 8.46 lbs. in 1965, as compared with 0.40 lbs. per capita in 1937.[21]

4. Processed meat has also increased on a per capita basis. In 1937, 3.2 lbs. of canned meat were consumed per capita whereas in 1965 this amount had increased to a yearly average of 11.6 lbs. per capita.[22]

In sum, the many technological innovations in processing and preserving food have had the general effect of increasing processed-food consumption and increasing food store sales.

An Analysis of Changing Consumer Buying Habits

Whether the supermarket altered customer shopping habits or whether customer shopping habits have altered supermarket methods of operation, lines carried, and services offered is a moot point. One evident relationship does appear significant. The American consumer has fondly embraced the concept of "simplified selling," the basis of which essentially is self-service and cash-and-carry merchandising introduced by supermarkets.

---

[19] U.S. Department of Agriculture, Agricultural Marketing Service, *Consumption of Food in the United States,* 1909-52. Data for 1965 to be found in U.S.D.A. *Statistical Bulletin No. 364,* Supplement for 1965, p. 20.

[20] *Ibid.,* pp. 10 and 11.

[21] *Ibid.,* pp. 9 and 12.

[22] *Ibid.,* pp. 5 and 14.

Changing Consumer Buying Habits

In discussing changes in buying habits the concern is principally with the "how," "when," and "where" of customer behavior.[23] The posing of these questions and the answers thereto can greatly aid a merchandiser in establishing and modifying store policies, methods, and procedures to meet best the needs and wants of his customers, and thus assure larger and more profitable sales.

A plethora of studies dealing with consumer buying habits have been conducted by advertising agencies, private research firms, universities, and the research departments of corporations, newspapers, and periodicals. No attempt will be made here to discuss the merits or findings of all these studies. However, the *Progressive Grocer* studies, which are perhaps as comprehensive, and which have been conducted for as long a period as any, will be looked at briefly.

Both the "Colonial Study" and the "Consumer Dynamics in the Super Market" study reveal interesting insights into supermarket shopping habits and attitudes. The highlights of these two studies follow, with a later elaboration on some of the more important findings.[24]

1. Women alone do 54 per cent of the family shopping in supermarkets. Two out of five shoppers are accompanied by men or children. For many families, shopping is becoming a family affair.

2. Today's shopper spends an average of 29 minutes per supermarket trip as compared with less than 18 minutes 10 years ago. This means in excess of 50 per cent more selling opportunity for the store operator.

3. Four out of five shoppers go to a supermarket at least twice a week. Over half go three or more times. This means that supermarkets are no longer getting just once-a-week shoppers, but that they are also getting much of the fill-in business.

4. Only one shopper in four has a completely written list. One in five has a partially written list. Of all customers, those using shopping-list reminders spend six minutes more and buy $2.22 more than customers who trust their memories to fill their carts with their needs.

---

[23] Charles F. Phillips and Delbert J. Duncan, *Marketing Principles and Methods* (Homewood, Illinois: Richard D. Irwin, Inc., 1956), p. 55.

[24] For a more expanded treatment of consumer behavior data, habits and attitudes, see the "Colonial Study," *Progressive Grocer*, 1963-1964, and "Consumer Dynamics in the Super Market," *Progressive Grocer*, Part I, October, 1965; Part II, November, 1965; Part III, December, 1965; Part IV, January, 1966; Part V, February, 1966; Part VI, March, 1966.

5. An average of 14 items are bought per shopping trip as compared with slightly more than 12 items five years ago. One shopper in three buys more than 15 items. Shoppers are spending 50 per cent more time and buying 8 per cent more merchandise.
6. Shopper purchases are substantial on every day of the week, although more purchases are made on week ends. Fridays and Saturdays are by far the busiest traffic days.
7. The average week-end customer spends $12.84 per shopping trip. The average purchase made by customers who shop less than 10 minutes is $3.67, while customers who spend over 40 minutes spend $22.02.

Additional information pertaining to the supermarket shopper follows.[25]

1. Three out of every four women shoppers are housewives, and one out of eight is a male head of household.
2. Eighty-five per cent of shoppers have at least some high school education. The majority have high school diplomas. American supermarket shoppers generally are intelligent, well-informed, discriminatory buyers.
3. The bulk of today's shoppers are in the age group 25 to 40 years.
4. Almost 60 per cent of the supermarket shoppers have family incomes of over $5,200 per year. Eight out of 10 have family incomes of at least $3,900.

The Increasing Incidence of Impulse Buying

Impulse buying is becoming a very prevalent practice among supermarket shoppers. Impulse buying is defined as a purchase resulting from a decision made on the spot in the outlet where the consumer sees the product displayed. Impulse buying is frequently divided into reminder buying and suggestion buying. Reminder buying occurs when a shopper sees a product and remembers that the stock at home is exhausted or low. Suggestion buying occurs when the buyer sees a product displayed and visualizes a need for it.

The tremendous growth of self-service merchandising by supermarkets and superette food stores has contributed to the growth of impulse buying.

In a recent study Kollat and Willett estimate that the average consumer makes 50.5 per cent of her supermarket purchases on an unplanned or impulse basis.[26] This study, however, raises some serious questions about the meaning and significance of impulse buying.

---

[25] *Ibid.*
[26] David T. Kollat and Ronald P. Willett, "Customer Impulse Purchasing Behavior," *Journal of Marketing Research,* February, 1967, pp. 21-31.

From these figures one might infer that in excess of 50 per cent of all supermarket purchases are unplanned, and that the consumer buyer to a considerable extent makes food purchases on an impulse basis. One writer argues with rather convincing logic that the shopper has already thought her purchase through, that she actually uses a systematic display as a shopping list, and that she will not buy an item if it is not on her list, either mental or written, and within the constraints of her budget.[27]

Nevertheless, there is little serious doubt about the supermarket's opportunity to sell a great deal of its merchandise on an impulse or unplanned basis or that the increase in impulse purchasing in recent years has not been of considerable magnitude. The cause of this increase can generally be attributed to increases in income, growth of self-service, and the increasingly large number of items stocked in supermarkets. Further, many impulse purchases can be attributed to the attractive displays of well-advertised brands and attractively packaged merchandise which permit customers to inspect visually many commodities.

The Supermarket As a One-Stop Shopping Center

Manufacturers and marketers must be constantly alert to the shifts in types of stores where customers dispense patronage. The American shopper is depending on the supermarket for more and more of the general merchandise lines she needs.

Items which were at one time purchased mainly in variety, department, or drug stores are now being merchandised quite successfully in supermarkets and superettes. For example, in 1952, 43.4 per cent of all women's hosiery sold in Philadelphia went through department stores, with an additional 21.8 per cent through women's specialty shops. By 1955, these percentages had fallen to 37.7 and 14.1 per cent, respectively, while the supermarket's share of this business had increased from 2.6 to 10.9 per cent.[28]

Naturally, as supermarkets widen their product lines, they concomitantly broaden, to a considerable extent, the nature of their appeal. In short, the probability that the supermarket will carry

---

[27] Gilbert Burck, "What Makes Women Buy?" *Fortune,* August, 1956, p. 174.
[28] "Non-Food Notes," *Super Market Merchandising,* November, 1955, p. 33.

an item of appeal to a given consumer increases as the breadth of line becomes wider and the product mix moves toward a greater assortment of general merchandise lines. This is exactly what has happened during the past several years. As a matter of fact, the supermarket is now an important outlet for such products as health and beauty aids, housewares, soft goods, magazines, toys, phonograph records, stationery and sewing needs. Interestingly enough, one recent study reports that the percentage of supermarkets carrying these respective items varies between 96 and 63 per cent.[29]

Other Changes in Buying Habits

Men today are playing a more important role in food and other buying for the family. This fact is accounted for quite likely by the shorter working hours which give these men more freedom for shopping and the increased proportion of women who work. Actually, the degree of influence exercised by the man as opposed to the woman of the household varies widely according to what is being purchased. As the food supermarket becomes more and more a general merchandise store, men are likely to play a more important role as supermarket shoppers. Women, however, remain the principal supermarket shoppers, although many merchants have already realized the necessity of appealing to both men and women.

Another example of changes taking place in consumer buying habits is the growing importance of night openings and the desire of many people to make purchases during evening hours and on Sundays. Consequently, many retail stores are now open a night or two each week and in some areas numerous supermarkets remain open on Sundays.

Summary

The thesis of this chapter is that certain environmental forces have generally tended to foster the growth and development of the supermarket. Because supermarkets, like other business institutions, operate within a business environment, the state of activity within this competitive or business milieu can and does greatly

---

[29] "Food Retailing Weathers Stormy Year with Best Sales Gains in Decade," Thirty-Fourth Annual Report of the Grocery Industry, *Progressive Grocer,* April, 1967.

affect the state of "health" of the business institution. Given favorable environmental factors, such as increasing population, favorable movements in population, rising incomes, and others, the business institution is more likely to grow, prosper, and expand. The relationships between demographic, economic, and technological forces and their effect on the growth of supermarkets were developed and analyzed. Finally, the changes in consumer buying habits and the effects of these changes on supermarket growth and development were investigated.

Chapter 4 | Trends in Supermarket Merchandising Strategies

WE HAVE seen that the main environmental forces affecting growth and development of supermarkets are population growth, rising incomes, changes in technology, and changes in consumer buying habits. The discussion of forces tending to favor growth and development of supermarkets is continued by looking now at those internal or management-initiated factors which have led to the relative success of supermarkets in their role as the nation's number-one distributor of food and grocery products.

The implications of the chapter title should be explored before proceeding further. The main consideration at this point is with merchandising trends. Historical developments are discussed only inasmuch as they contribute to the enlightenment and understanding of the current situation. The word "merchandising," although a part of the marketing literature and vocabulary for some time, is frequently used in a loose and ambiguous manner unless specifically defined. The intent here is to use the term to mean " . . . the planning involved in marketing the right merchandise or service at the right place, at the right time, in the right quantities, and at the right price."[1]

Therefore, breaking down the elements of a firm's merchandising strategy into the various "mix" components becomes an easy task. The total merchandising strategy becomes an over-all plan of attack to enable the firm to reach predetermined objectives. Oxenfeldt has stated the problem in a similar manner. He says a (merchandising) strategy consists of two parts: (1) the definition of marketing

---

[1] "Report of the A.M.A. Definitions Committee," *Journal of Marketing*, October, 1948.

targets; and (2) the composition of a (merchandising) mix—picking a combination of devices that will be employed.[2]

The combinations of devices available to a supermarket which will enable the firm to seek its desired objectives are generally found within five broad categories. These are price policies or appeals, promotional policies and tactics, product policies, buying policies, and location policies. Some stores will attempt to maximize their competitive advantage via the astute manipulation of all five variables in their merchandising mix, while others will attempt to build an image based upon only one or two of these variables. In other words, some firms may choose to compete with a vigorous price appeal, and they may further strive to project this price image via an aggressive advertising campaign. They may also integrate backward in order to obtain lower buying prices. Still other firms may wish to compete outside the realm of the price arena. These firms may choose to hold up prices and project an image via advertising of high quality and personal service. The particular manner in which a firm decides to execute its merchandising strategy and the particular concentration of variables the firm employs will largely determine its success or failure in the market place.

There can be little doubt concerning the need for a sound merchandising strategy for supermarket firms. The rapid expansion of supermarkets (new openings) sparks vigorous competition within the industry. In 1965, newly opened supermarkets represented 9 per cent of all units in operation at the end of the year.[3]

Competition from other forms of retailing is making gradual but marked inroads into what was once considered the private domain of the supermarkets. In 1960, the Super Market Institute, in a survey among its members, asked the following question: "Are you getting severe competition in your retail food operation from outlets that are not primarily food stores?" One out of every four companies, including firms in all size groups and in all regions, answered "yes."

[2] Alfred R. Oxenfeldt, "The Formulation of a Market Strategy," *Managerial Marketing: Perspectives and Viewpoints,* eds. E. Kelly and W. Lazar (Homewood, Illinois: Richard D. Irwin, Inc., 1958), p. 267.

[3] Super Market Institute, *The Super Market Industry Speaks,* Eighteenth Annual Report (Chicago: Super Market Institute, 1966), p. 15.

In total, 8 per cent of the Super Market Institute member stores were in severe competition with other types of business. What types of business are the source of this competition? Discount houses, both open- and closed-door membership stores, were cited most frequently, followed by Army and Navy commissaries, farmer's markets, freezer plans, and variety stores. Two years previously, when the same question was asked of the Super Market Institute members, 9 per cent of the companies reported severe competition from other outlets, affecting a total of only 2½ per cent of the supermarkets.[4]

In discussing the extent of competition facing new supermarkets opened in 1965, the Super Market Institute reports that the typical new supermarket opened in 1965 is confronted with nearby competition from three other sizable food stores (two supermarkets and one superette), with a combined selling area of 28,000 square feet and estimated weekly sales of $60,000. Further, the larger stores encounter more severe competition. The supermarkets in new larger shopping centers tend to face the greatest amount of competition, while units in new small shopping centers have the least amount. But in every type of location, the new supermarkets are contending with abundant competition.[5]

Thus, supermarket operators are being faced with an ever-greater challenge to formulate sound but dynamic and aggressive merchandising strategies in order to maintain their dominant competitive position.

The development of sound merchandising strategies rests with management. In larger chain organizations, these responsibilities may be centralized in a regional or main office of the organization. The task of the individual store manager then becomes one of instituting and implementing this strategy in the most effective manner. In the independent supermarket, the store manager's and/or owner's responsibility is broadened, for the manager must develop merchandise strategy policies as well as implement them. The voluntary wholesalers have played an important role in aiding

---

[4] *Ibid.,* p. 15.

[5] "Facts about New Super Markets Opened in 1965," *Eighteenth Annual Report,* Super Market Institute, 1966, p. 10.

the independent store manager in formulating highly effective strategies.

There is frequently no one particular objective of a supermarket. The objective may be to have the largest store in the area, to make a stated percentage of profits on sales, to achieve the "average" sales per square foot for this size store, or to attain other goals.

Many firms, however, admit that if one primary objective is to be sought, this objective should be profit. The question immediately then becomes: "What profit?" The concept of profitability must be linked to some base if one is to establish a usable criterion. Long-run profit as a return on investment is the accepted base.[6] Merchandising strategies should thus be evaluated by supermarket management in light of the opposing contributions to total profit made available by the alternative courses of action.

The analysis of trends in supermarket merchandising strategies is now undertaken. The examination of these strategies will be made in terms of the following key variables:

(1) Product and inventory policies.
(2) Buying policies.
(3) Pricing policies.
(4) Promotion policies.
(5) Location policies.

Trends in Product and Inventory Policies

During recent years, the number of consumers of food and nonfood products has increased, the income of these consumers has risen, technological developments have brought forth an increasing number of products suitable for sale through food supermarkets, and customers' tastes and behavior have changed significantly so that new food and nonfood products are being demanded by supermarket shoppers. In an attempt to keep pace, the supermarket has constantly modified its product and inventory policies.

There are several additional reasons why supermarkets continue to broaden their product mix. First, if the industry is to maintain its

---

[6] The Super Market Institute is doing a commendable job of educating its members to this profit criterion. See for instance, "The Changing Times," *Proceedings of the Mid-Year Conference,* Super Market Institute, January, 1962, p. 10.

share of the consumer dollar, the addition of new food items is necessary. Second, the American consumer has usually responded favorably to innovations in food technology and processing. Convenience foods such as frozen food, cake mixes, and dehydrated potatoes have met with enthusiastic customer acceptance. And, finally, the supermarket operator, in his constant search for new sales and profit opportunities, simply could not afford to bypass the increased business from new food product sales.

Not only have supermarkets throughout the postwar period continued to increase the absolute number of food lines, but inventories have tended to become much more diversified by including many general merchandise or nonfood products.

The following figures illustrate that supermarkets have more than doubled the number of items carried during the period from 1946 to 1966:[7]

Year	Items
1946	3,000
1950	3,750
1955	4,723
1957	5,144
1958	5,600
1959	5,800
1960	6,000
1961	6,300
1962	6,600
1963	6,800
1964	6,900
1965	7,100
1966	7,250

The 7,250 items stocked by the average supermarket in 1966 can be grouped by departments under seven major headings. Several studies have been undertaken in an effort to evaluate the relative importance of each of these departments.

Table 4.1 shows that some changes have occurred throughout recent years in the percentage of sales attributed to each of these product classes. In the main, the relative changes have been slight.

---

[7] Annual Reports, *Progressive Grocer,* for years shown.

TABLE 4.1

PERCENTAGE OF SALES OF MAJOR PRODUCT CLASSIFICATIONS
TRANSACTED BY SUPERMARKETS

(results of four leading studies)

Product Class	Food Town Study	Super Value Study	Dillon Study	Colonial Study
Meats	28.11%	22.42%	21.90%	24.09%
Dairy Products	8.61	11.51	11.08	9.34
Bakery Products	2.67	5.76	6.23	4.63
Frozen Foods	4.14	4.78	3.50	3.75
Produce	12.76	8.79	10.00	6.80
Grocery Items	39.49	43.68	42.60	45.78
Nonfoods	4.22	3.06	4.69	5.61
Total	100.0%	100.0%	100.0%	100.0%

Sources: "The Food Town Study," *Progressive Grocer,* January, 1955.

"How an Average Customer Spends Her Super Market Dollars—Super Value Markets," *Facts in Grocery Distribution,* 26th Annual Survey, *Progressive Grocer,* April, 1959, p. F20.

"Where Sales and Profits Come From—the Dillon Company," *Progressive Grocer,* 1960, p. D6.

"Colonial Study Data Can Help Improve Store Operations," *Progressive Grocer,* November, 1963, p. C43.

Influx of New Food Items

A most recent *Progressive Grocer* study indicates that a typical supermarket may be offered 125 new or improved items a week, or about 6,500 a year. From these offerings, 800 may be added to the super's inventory mix. In the course of a year, however, the same store would typically drop 600 items, for a net gain of 200 items.[8]

During the course of the field interviewing to gather primary research data for this original study, the question was put to 20 top food executives, "What percentage of products handled by supermarkets today would you estimate were not handled five years ago?" The range of estimates varied from 20 to 50 per cent.

The president of one food chain said this:

[8] "New Products: $11 Billion New Businesses since 1954," *Progressive Grocer,* April, 1965, pp. 101-106.

An inventory taken today compared to one taken five years ago would show that 50 per cent of the items on supermarket shelves right now are new and improved items. The same condition will probably hold equally true five years from now.[9]

The rapid growth and the influx of new products are constantly forcing supermarket operators to scrutinize carefully their product and inventory policies, including such elements as space allocation and utilization, brand decisions, and the ever-growing question, "how to merchandise non-foods?"

Theoretically, from 1954 to 1965, had the typical supermarket operator not stocked new food items to satisfy current consumer wants, he could have witnessed approximately a 22 per cent decrease in business, assuming no other factors contributed to an increase or decrease in volume.[10]

Space Allocation and Utilization

Many problems have been created for the supermarket which stem from the rapid growth of new and expanding food lines. The problem of accepting or rejecting a new product is no simple task. Food executives interviewed in this study agreed almost unanimously that there is no simple (or workable complex) system or device which will aid them in screening new products. One respondent stated: "It's a wholly subjective matter. No matter what we have tried the procedure generally boils down to one thing: the subjective opinion of one or more individuals."[11]

Supermarket operators are quite disgruntled with the tendency of many manufacturers simply to duplicate existing products and then ask for space and shelf facings. However, those products are eagerly embraced which can gain a consumer franchise and pay for the shelf space occupied by making an adequate contribution to profit.

Another respondent interviewed stated that: "We are expanding the number of our merchandise offerings. Some sellers accuse us of dropping a product for every new product we take on. They

---

[9] *Ibid.*, p. 101.
[10] *Ibid.*, p. 101.
[11] Interview with R. Yohers, Vice President and General Manager, Foodland Markets, Seattle, Washington, Winter, 1961.

even try to suggest to us what products we should drop. And you can believe it isn't one of theirs."[12]

Between 1959 and 1965, chains, voluntaries, and cooperatives added 3,200 items and dropped 2,100, for a gain of 1,100 items. Each year 220 new items were added to supermarket shelves. This means that 5,300 decisions were involved concerning what items to add and discontinue.[13]

Inadequate shelf space, as well as the proper allocation of space to existing products, must be considered when making decisions affecting new products. Close scrutiny will invariably uncover items that are not producing their share of sales.

The Dillon Study pointed up such inequities in unit sales of items within product groups as these: in the canned fruit department four out of 11 items were producing 84 per cent of unit sales for canned cherries; two out of five items were producing 84 per cent of unit sales in applesauce. In the canned vegetable group, 10 of 21 corn items accounted for 81 per cent of unit sales; 12 of 21 items accounted for 81 per cent of green bean units.[14] These figures vividly indicate the need for periodic evaluation of the importance of individual items to the basic variety being offered, in terms of the facings they occupy.

Those items that rank high in terms of unit sales are not always the same as those which rank highest in dollar sales and rank in gross margin per unit. Table 4.2, showing information taken from *Progressive Grocer's* Colonial Study, should demonstrate this point.

Two important aspects can be noted from Table 4.2: (1) eight of the leading 15 unit producers fall among the leading dollar sales producers, and (2) only two fall within the top 15 gross margin per-unit producers. This example should demonstrate to some extent one basic supermarket pricing concept: high unit sales, low unit profit; low unit sales, high unit profit.

Supermarket operators can be greatly aided in formulating effective product and inventory policies as a part of their total mer-

---

[12] Interview with James Bidwell, Manager of the Indiana Grocers Co-operative Association, Summer, 1961.

[13] "New Products: $11 Billion New Businesses since 1954," *op. cit.,* p. 101.

[14] "The Dillon Study," *Progressive Grocer,* June, 1960, pp. D20-21.

TABLE 4.2

How Leaders in Unit Sales Rank in Dollar Sales and Gross Margin per Unit

Commodity	Rank in Unit Sales	Rank in Dollar Sales	Rank in Gross Margin per Unit
Canned, Powdered Milk	1	25	46
Sugar	2	15	49
Soap	3	16	38
Cigarettes	4	1	50
Paper Products	5	3	21
Beer	6	12	47
Canned Fruit	7	9	14
Dried Fruit	8	40	8
Pet Foods	9	21	23
Soft Drinks	10	10	37
Hand, Face Soaps	11	36	40
Canned Vegetables	12	5	15
Canned Fish	13	35	34
Dried Vegetables	14	38	32
Crackers, Cookies	15	6	22

Source: "A Statistical Profile of the Modern Super Market—the Colonial Study," *Progressive Grocer,* October, 1963, pp. C18-C19.

chandising strategies by adhering to a few well-founded merchandising principles:[15]

1. Don't expect to sell cases and cases of products. Nine out of ten items sell less than one case per week.
2. Order according to movement. Too little on hand means out of stock, lost sales. Too much means tied up inventory—cash that could work better elsewhere.
3. Look for new items. A large percentage of store profits is coming from items not in existence 10 years ago.
4. Dispossess the shelf warmers. A thorough examination of items may show that many items are not carrying their share of the load.
5. Face by volume of sales. Use profit and unit figures to select facings. Big sellers, more facings. Shelves won't sell down as quickly.
6. Position items by unit sales. In larger product groups place big unit sellers at opposite ends where practical, to pull traffic through the department.
7. Position on shelves by volume. Use combination dollar sales-units to arrive at decision.

---

[15] *Ibid.,* pp. 34-35.

Of these above-listed rules or principles, numbers 5 and 7 may warrant further elaboration inasmuch as they unquestionably offer the best solution to the perplexing problem of proper space allocation and utilization which in turn may lead to greatest dollar profits.

Facing by Volume of Sales. Space allocation is largely a matter of determining proper facings for individual brands and sizes of every item in the grocery department.

In most situations, this decision amounts to a minimum facing situation determined by the item's pack and the capacity for facing on the shelf. However, experience has shown that large, fast-moving items should be given at least the optimum amount of shelf space. Some operators have attempted to slight fast-moving, high-demand items in terms of space, reasoning that these items would continue to move off shelves at a rapid pace, in turn making their contribution to profits, while carrying the burden of reduced shelf space. Such has not been the case.[16] Sales records indicate that in the typical supermarket doing a volume of $1,000,000 to $2,000,000 per year, 90 per cent of the items handled sell less than 24 units per week. Therefore, the majority of items—especially the big-volume items—should be allocated enough facings to stock a case and a half of merchandise so that out-of-stocks will be minimized and full case restocking facilitated.

It is important to remember that an increase or decrease in space allocated to a product group will undoubtedly affect its sales so that return per dollar invested and turnover cannot be precisely predicted. The critical fact to remember is that both these performance criteria are dependent on a variable (shelf space) that, although planned carefully, is difficult to manage in any one store.

Position on Shelves by Volume. Progressive Grocer, as a result of several of its published studies, has long been advocating this criterion as a good solution to the shelf-positioning problems. These efforts have generally been well recognized and received, but many operators still fail to see the logic of this device. However, some retailers feature the item with the highest percentage margin. This is unacceptable because mere percentage margin can be worse than

---

[16] *Ibid.,* p. D37.

meaningless. The most acceptable decision rule appears to be to give the best position to the items that earn the greatest number of gross profit dollars per square foot.

Here is what actually happened when the two decision rules were applied in actual store tests:[17]

How Proper Facings and Position Affect Total Category Sales and Profits

	Per Cent Gain Sales	Per Cent Gain Gross Profit
Canned vegetables	+ 5	+ 6
Canned meat	+35	+44
Canned fish	+57	+49

The test was conducted in the three above-named departments. A sales audit of each item in each department was taken over a four-week period.

With the information from the sales audit, each item was refaced according to unit sales and preferred shelf height given to the item that earned the most gross profit dollars. After the resetting, two weeks were allowed to elapse in order to enable customers to get acquainted with the new arrangement. A sales audit taken after the next four weeks showed these results: sales up from 5 to 57 per cent; gross profit up 6 to 49 per cent.

As a result of similar studies, many firms are now turning to this theory and finding higher volume and profit when each item is faced and positioned according to merit.

Trends in Brand Decisions and Policies

From the point of view of the supermarket operator, the question of whether to promote and merchandise manufacturer's brands or distributor brands is indeed an important issue and one which greatly affects the over-all marketing strategy of the firm. Not only must the operator weigh the various advantages and disadvantages of stocking one type of brand as opposed to the other, but he must usually decide what proportion of his total product mix will be composed of manufacturer's brands and to what extent he wishes to merchandise private or distributor brands. Before proceeding

---

[17] "Where We Stand Today in Private Brand Merchandising," *Progressive Grocer,* August, 1959, p. 6. See also, "Shelf Altitudes Affect Buying Attitudes," *Progressive Grocer,* March, 1964, pp. C127-129.

further, however, a distinction must be made between these two types of brands.

Originally, and in many cases today, brands were classified as national or private. The former were owned by manufacturers, and the latter were owned by wholesalers or retailers. This distinction has proved to be awkward. Since many manufacturers are not national sellers, a more appropriate nomenclature would be to call manufacturer's brands those brands owned by producers and manufacturers. The industry itself, however, is not quite so academically precise. Realizing the imperfections of the terms "national" and "private," the trade continues to employ the terms in discussion of brand policies. Therefore, in order that various industry studies and sources can be utilized, the terms national and private will continue to be used.

The story of brands is a colorful chapter in the history of marketing. Briefly stated, private (distributor) brands were the first to emerge and long reigned as the most powerful and influential branding force in the food field. The improvement in mass communications enabled many manufacturers to build strong allegiance to their own brands, and private (distributor) brands rapidly dwindled in number.[18] The depression, however, by shrinking purchasing power, gave new impetus to consumer demand for lower prices which distributors were able to obtain through private brands without a large promotional burden. Private brands continued to exercise a strong consumer appeal until the outbreak of World War II, which brought about two conditions disadvantageous to private brands: merchandise shortages and increased consumer purchasing power. Throughout the postwar period, these two conditions continued to hamper the growth and development of private brand merchandising.[19] However, since about 1955, supermarkets have been faced with a number of situations which have caused many of them to re-evaluate their merchandising plans and policies pertaining to private vs. national brands.

---

[18] Nugent Wedding, "Contemporary Brand Policies," *Frontiers in Marketing Thought,* contributed papers, conference of the American Marketing Association (Bloomington, Indiana: Indiana University, December, 1954), pp. 145-56.

[19] See Cole, *et al., Manufacturer and Distributor Brands,* Bulletin Series: No. 80 (Urbana, Illinois: University of Illinois, 1955).

Since about 1955, food retailing has caught up with its expansion goals, and there has been no shortage of good, aggressive, modern supermarkets. New supermarkets opened after 1956 could no longer expect to draw appreciable trade from smaller stores and had to pull business away from existing supermarkets. Competition has been gradually increasing among supermarkets, bringing forth such cost-increasing devices as giveaways, trading stamps, and premium plans. In order to combat this stringent competition and to avoid direct price competition with other operators, many supermarkets have begun turning once again to private brands.

In a rather extensive survey conducted by Selling Research, Inc., among supermarket executives, 19 per cent of those interviewed had immediate plans for moving into private labels in one or more lines.[20]

Some firms are introducing private brands into their product and merchandise strategies at the rate of one new private label per week in the belief that private brands are the answer to sagging profits and stiffer competition.[21] Other operators are looking more receptively toward private brands because of the freedom and flexibility of private brand merchandising. Some operators are dissatisfied with the rigors of national brands. Claims are made that national brand manufacturers are too insistent on overfacings, that margins are too low, and that customers are gradually rebelling against higher-priced national brands.[22]

There are, of course, arguments both pro and con for private as well as national brands. Without presenting an exhaustive list, the logic of the argument is essentially this: national brands are generally highly advertised by the manufacturer. In essence, these brands are said to be presold to the consumer, thus making them less costly for the retailer himself to merchandise. On the other hand, because of the high promotional cost incurred by the manufacturer, margins to the retailer are generally smaller than margins

---

[20] "Own Label Additions Slated by 19% in Poll," *Super Market News,* August 1, 1960, p. 4.

[21] "Once-a-Week Label Introduction," *Super Market News,* February 1, 1960, p. 1.

[22] "Private Labels Termed Sales Asset," *Super Market News,* February 29, 1960, p. 4.

on private brands and the price to the consumer is somewhat higher on national than on private brands.

Private brands afford the retailer a somewhat more flexible merchandising approach. The store has more assurance of repeat patronage if the customer accepts his private brands. The retailer is relieved of direct price comparison with his use of private brands, his pricing policies can be somewhat more flexible, and, further, the private brand frequently offers the retailer a higher markup.

The big chains have ready capital with which to invest in their own private brands. The regional chains have a growing but not an intense interest in private brands. Most of these regional chains have achieved their growth by promoting national brands. Voluntaries and cooperatives are the fastest-growing elements in all food distribution, but they do not appear eager to move to private brands. It is unlikely that the unaffiliated independents will ever become seriously interested in, or become strong supporters of, private brands.

The merchandising policy question or decision of whether to promote private or national brands and the mix to employ if both are used cannot be satisfactorily answered. The solution, of course, rests with the individual operator, his competitive position, his merchandising goals or objectives, and other management policies. Private brands still appear to be decidedly the less important of the two, and most evidence continues to support the belief that national brands will remain the dominant factor in most supermarket operators' branding policies.

Product Lines Vulnerable to Private Labels. Private brands become successful generally in those product lines which have contained a large consumer franchise and thus the potential for volume sales. By dividing groceries into three general categories, the discovery was made that only in the one category of high sales-volume products was there an appreciable number of private brands. The general rule is that the product must move at a rate of about 11 units a week before private brands can successfully compete with national brands. Most retailers are adding private labels in the high-frequency items such as soaps, detergents, canned juices, and frozen foods.

A staff report of the National Commission on Food Marketing developed in cooperation with the National Association of Food Chains revealed that in a breakdown of nine major product classifications based on reports from 113 retail respondents, private brand volume ranged from a low of 26.2 per cent of sales for canned vegetables and 30 to 35 per cent for canned fruit, weiners, and coffee, to just under 50 per cent for bacon, frozen fruits, and vegetables and slightly over 50 per cent for dairy and bakery products.[23]

The Importance of Private Brands in Terms of Grocery Items Handled. That the bulk of most supermarket grocery inventories are composed of national brands is certainly no secret. However, that private-brand items comprise such a small percentage of the total items may come as some surprise.

One *Progressive Grocer* study revealed the following:

Number of Private Brand Items Handled
(Groceries and Frozen Foods)

	Number Private Brand Items	Per Cent of All Grocery and Frozen Food Items
Big chain	446	10
Regional chain	165	4
Voluntary group	229	6

As can be observed, the number of private-brand items turns out to be lower than generally expected, and one might wonder whether the sheer number of private-brand items is not frequently overestimated.

Price Differential between Private and National Brands

Using $1.00 as the average price of all national brands, the price of similar merchandise under the private label would be $.83 in the big chain, $.86 in the regional chain, and $.92 in the store belonging to the voluntary or cooperative. In general, the private brand needs price advantages equal to or greater than these averages in order to gain acceptance from consumers.

---

[23] "Organization and Competition in Food Retailing," Technical Study No. 7, National Commission on Food Marketing (June, 1966), pp. 129-139.

These findings of the *Progressive Grocer* study are now briefly summarized.[24]

	National Brand	Private Brand	Private Brand Per Cent Lower
Big chain	$1.00	$ .83	17
Regional chain	1.00	.86	14
Voluntary cooperative	1.00	.92	8

The per cent of dollar sales of private vs. national brands showed that national brands account for nearly 92 per cent of dollar sales in all categories. However, in terms of per cent gross profit the private brands made a better showing in this study, accounting for about 23 per cent of the total.

There is little doubt that the competition between nationally advertised food brands and private labels has been intense for a considerable number of years. There is even more evidence to suggest that the battle will increase in scope and intensity. One recent nontrade-affiliated study suggests that private label foods are growing in importance for many reasons—the efforts of manufacturers of nationally advertised brands notwithstanding.[25] These authors suggest that a key factor is the development of giant retailing, in which relatively few corporate and contract chains account for a sizable share of total retail food sales. Their principal argument is that this growing concentration will trigger a dramatic surge toward the use of private labels in the years ahead.

Without question, part of the success of private brand merchandising lies with the consumer. Where the difference between purchase price of advertised and private label products is substantial, retailers can bear the cost of handling duplicate items and still sell private labels to consumers profitably at lower prices. Retailer brands, as has been shown, almost always sell at lower prices because at equal prices, consumers appear to prefer national brands. Thus, private labels offer the consumer an alternative to paying for the cost of advertising and promoting national brands.[26]

---

[24] "Where We Stand Today in Private Brand Merchandising," *op. cit.,* pp. 1-6.

[25] Harper W. Boyd, Jr., and Ronald Frank, "The Importance of Private Labels in Food Retailing," *Business Horizons* (Summer, 1966), pp. 81-91.

[26] "Food from Farmer to Consumer," *Report of the National Commission on Food Marketing,* U.S. Government Printing Office (June, 1966), pp. 75-76.

Trends in General Merchandise Policies

The supermarket is essentially a food store. Yet in the postwar period, especially since about 1954, nonfood items (or what are more typically referred to today as general merchandise items) have accounted for a larger and larger share of supermarket sales. General merchandise sales account for between 5 and 8 per cent of total supermarket volume.[27] This figure has been gradually increasing during recent years. In 1954, general merchandise sales as a per cent of total supermarket sales were estimated at 3.5 per cent; in 1956 at 5.0 per cent; in 1958 at 5.0 per cent; in 1960 at 5.4 per cent; and in 1966 at 6.0 per cent.[28]

There are several important questions pertaining to merchandise strategies and product policies which arise in the minds of supermarket managers when discussing the issue of general merchandise policies. Essentially these questions, from the point of view of the individual operator, boil down to these:

1. How much space for nonfoods?
2. How many items?
3. Who will supply them?
4. How much volume from them?
5. How much profit from their sale?

The first two of these questions are in many respects highly individual and involve technical considerations that must be answered within the framework of each store's operations. Some research has been completed which answers in part these questions.[29]

The interest here is to explore the question of general merchandise lines from several important aspects. The most important question of all would appear to be: Why have so many supermarkets moved into nonfood or general merchandise lines? And, secondly: What appears to be the major trend in general merchandise lines

---

[27] This figure may not reflect adequately the amount of "nonfood" items being sold by supermarkets for essentially two reasons: first, there exists the definitional problem as to just what constitutes "nonfoods" or general merchandise lines. Soaps, detergents, cleaning supplies, and many other items are clearly nonfood items; yet they are reported as food sales. Second, the above figures are averages for the two different-sized supermarkets as defined by *Progressive Grocer* and the Super Market Institute, respectively.

[28] These figures are near approximations taken from both *Progressive Grocer* and Super Market Institute annual published reports.

[29] See for instance, "The Dillon Study" and "The Colonial Study" of *Progressive Grocer.*

in supermarkets? The discussion, therefore, will focus primarily on these central issues.

General merchandise lines normally have fallen into eight merchandise categories. These are: health and beauty aids, housewares, hardware, soft goods, magazines, toys, records, and stationery. Health and beauty aids are by far the most important of these categories in terms of dollar sales. This classification is admittedly somewhat arbitrary inasmuch as new general merchandise lines are being introduced into supermarket selling programs at a very rapid rate.

When the writer put this question, "Do you believe more, or less, general merchandise lines will be added in supermarkets during the next 3 to 5 years?" to 20 executives associated directly with supermarket operation, the overwhelming response was "more." Such items as auto accessories, summer furniture, lumber supplies, infant needs other than baby foods, and complete sporting goods departments are just a sampling of those new lines mentioned as being susceptible to adoption by supermarket operations.

Why General Merchandise Lines?

Supermarket operators who have gone in heavily for merchandising nonfood lines state unanimously that the reason they sell nonfoods is to satisfy the demands of their customers. True as this may be, the reasons lie much deeper than this superficial statement. Ventures into nonfoods are not being undertaken by only a few offbeat stores, but by a growing number of the nation's top food retailing chains. In some cases, the diverse goods and services are offered in stores that look much like conventional supermarkets. In others, however, supermarket chains are opening big "combination" stores which merely have food departments. These activities reflect not just a supermarket diversification drive, but something akin to a grocery store revolution which in many instances is turning supermarkets into modernized versions of the general stores from which they evolved.[30]

There are a host of reasons both pro and con for adding or not adding nonfood lines. Generally speaking, nonfood items are added

---

[30] See Chapter 5.

if they have merchandising and purchasing characteristics which are similar to profitable food items. For example, nonfood items which have a low unit price, high frequency of purchase, and fast turnover, involving routine reordering procedures, quick identification, and no slow-down problems at the checkout, are likely to be viewed as likely candidates for inclusion in the product mix. On the other hand, products not possessing these characteristics and with which buyers lack familiarity are not too likely to receive favorable attention or inclusion.

The main reason, however, for many ventures into broadened general merchandise lines is the highly competitive nature of the supermarket business. Operators have literally been forced to broaden their product lines to include items which carry a more comfortable price margin. Tightening competition, rising costs, and falling profit margins have been the general rule on most of the supermarkets' conventional food lines. The number of supermarkets has nearly doubled in the last eight years, to around 35,000 in 1966. Because the nation's population has not grown nearly as rapidly, the average market for each supermarket has dwindled to 1,413 families in 1966, from 3,014 in 1950. And these families did not raise their food expenditures fast enough to maintain sales volume for all the stores. The average American household spent slightly less than $29.00 a week for food in 1966, about 10 cents more than in 1952.[31]

One answer to the tightening competitive situation was to take advantage of store traffic to sell the visiting shopper additional items or services. Nonfoods typically have larger gross margins than general food lines. One study, previously quoted, compared nonfoods with grocery averages and reported the following results.[32]

	All Nonfoods	Colonial Study Grocery Average
Per cent of total store sales	5.61	45.78
Percentage of linear floor feet	12%	69%
Linear floor feet	492.00	2,920.80
Weekly sales	$2,489.00	$20,319.00
Return per 100 dollars invested	$5.72	$4.84

[31] Computed from data shown in Chapter 3 exhibits.
[32] "A Statistical Profile of the Modern Supermarket," *Progressive Grocer,* October, 1963, pp. C16-C17.

Weekly dollar margin	$729.00	$3,905.00
Weekly dollar sales per linear foot	$5.05	$6.96
Dollar margin per linear floor foot	$1.48	$1.34
Dollar sales per item per week	$2.32	$5.55
Average profit per item per week	$0.18	$0.06

Supermarkets with their basic food lines are able to exert tremendous pulls on customer traffic. The preceding figures dramatize quite vividly the food store operators' desire, however, to merchandise successfully a large number of nonfood items.

What's New in General Merchandise Lines in Supermarkets?

Table 4.3 shows the percentage of supermarkets carrying given general merchandise lines.

New general merchandise lines are constantly finding their way into more and more supermarkets. The three leading lines both in terms of sales and profit contribution are health and beauty aids, housewares, and women's hosiery. General merchandise lines that appear to be gaining popularity in supermarkets are hardware, underwear, notions and soft goods, while photographic supplies and greeting cards are also growing in importance.

The merchandise line that is receiving careful attention from many supermarket merchandisers is soft goods. One midwestern

TABLE 4.3

SALES OF SELECTED NONFOOD LINES AND PERCENTAGE
OF SUPERMARKETS SELLING THESE SELECTED LINES

(sales in billions)

Commodity	1963	1964	1965	1966	Per Cent of Supers Handling, 1966
Health and beauty aids	$1.675	$1.800	$1.960	$2.160	96
Housewares	.560	.620	.675	.750	85
Soft goods	.245	.260	.275	.275	55
Magazines	.160	.175	.195	.210	69
Toys	.090	.095	.110	.115	68
Phonograph records	.070	.070	.070	.070	39
Stationery	.070	.075	.085	.095	82
Sewing needs	N.A.	N.A.	N.A.	.035	63
Total	$2.870	$3.095	$3.370	$3.710	

Source: *Progressive Grocer,* Annual Reports for years shown.

supermarket supplier executive made this comment: "There is no ceiling on soft good sales through supermarkets. The only ceiling is family buying power." "In other words," he went on to explain, "as family buying power increases, shoppers logically trade up in the type and number of apparel and accessory items they might buy in a supermarket. Many other leading nonfood items, of course, have a limited potential imposed by a fixed rate of use."[33]

Sources of Supply for Nonfoods

Food Topics undertook a two-year study on nonfoods under the direction of Dr. William Bonwich. Several trends pertaining to supermarket sources of supply for nonfoods are summarized from that study.[34] More companies make their nonfoods purchases from rack jobbers than from wholesalers or manufacturers. The percentage of companies for which the rack jobber is the major supplier ranges from a low of 27 per cent for garden supplies to a high of 85 per cent for phonograph records. Over three out of four companies get their major supplies of toys and housewares from the rack jobber.

Wholesalers are the most important source of supply for photographic supplies, garden supplies, and electrical appliances. For garden supplies, women's hosiery, glassware, and greeting cards, direct buying is relatively most significant. Generally, the larger the company, the more willing and the greater the inclination to buy direct. However, companies of all sizes use rack jobbers as their major source of supply for some items.

Trends in Supermarket Pricing Policies

The supermarket emerged in the early 1930's as a low-cost method of distributing food. The pricing strategy and philosophy of the early supermarkets conformed closely to the names of many of these early institutions, *i.e.,* the "price crusher" and the "price wrecker." Great emphasis was placed on price by these early supermarkets in an effort to draw traffic and establish themselves as

---

[33] Interview with Marsh Blackburn, Owner-manager, Hoosier Brokerage Co., Indianapolis, Indiana, Summer, 1961.
[34] William Bonwich, "Study of General Merchandise," *Food Topics,* March, 1960, p. 6.

truly low-price sellers. However, during the war years with the resultant merchandise shortages, price was abandoned to a certain extent as the basic appeal of the supermarket. Even long after the war was over, merchandise shortages continued which enabled supers to hold up prices while they attempted to enhance their competitive positions via better physical plants and services. The general effect of price cutting is to reduce marketing margins; service competition, however, tends to increase such margins.

Before proceeding further into our discussion of trends in supermarket pricing policies, let us examine several of the economic and environmental forces which would tend to affect the operator's pricing decisions.

Market Structure

Models of economic theory are of importance in pricing considerations for firms and industries for a number of reasons. Foremost of these is that economic theory aids the decision maker in selecting concepts of demand, competition, and cost which are relevant to the pricing problem under consideration. Once a body of these generalizations has been drawn which is pertinent to a type or group of economic or marketing decisions such as price, it is embodied in a concept known as market structure. Some diversity still exists which impedes the classification of supermarkets into a logic-tight market structure: size of firms differs widely—even the industry itself cannot quite decide what constitutes a supermarket in terms of volume requirements; the types of products offered, as well as the number of products offered, vary markedly; and spatial considerations and diversities are great.

Given a reasonably close examination of the literature, almost any desired classification of retail markets can be found. Stigler classifies nearly all such markets in the competitive sector.[35] Most of the English writers have described retailing as imperfect competition, or monopolistic competition. Smith finds the "imperfect divisibility" of retail units, "imperfect imputation of selling costs,"

---

[35] George J. Stigler, *Five Lectures on Economic Problems* (New York: The Macmillan Co., 1950), p. 57.

limited spatial monopoly, and the uninformed nature of the buyer to be strong imperfections afflicting retail markets.[36]

Others have suggested that oligopoly may be an important form in retailing:[37]

> It is inherent in this situation that conditions of oligopoly may arise at any time. By oligopoly is meant a situation in which the seller, in determining his price and output policy, takes into account the probable reactions to changes in his policy.

And, indeed, the temptation to embrace Lady Hall's comment is all but overwhelming, especially in regard to supermarkets. However, Hood and Yamey take critical exception to this position:[38]

> The use of an oversimplified theory of oligopoly is . . . unrealistic. Freedom of entry and chain linking of markets make it unwise to rely upon a mere counting of numbers. Tacit or formal agreements are not the simple arrangements which some theories suggest.

Holton argues that supermarkets are essentially oligopolists by stating that:[39]

> Retaliation does not take the form of retaliation on the identical item which the competition is featuring . . . for this is price competition of the clearest sort and anathema to the oligopolist.

Bob Holdren is rather contemptuous of this view and argues forcefully, but not necessarily convincingly, that supermarkets are not oligopolists, but, at most, monopolistically competitive.[40]

While the authorities differ as to the extent of interdependence among supermarkets, or as to whether or not the firms are monopolistic competitors or oligopolists, empirical evidence strongly suggests that the degree of interdependence is rather large. What appears to be important is that historically and presently most supermarkets tend to behave as oligopolists. Price elasticities are certainly substantial among supermarkets, and the brunt of any competitive move is usually borne by the geographically closest

---

[36] Henry Smith, *Retail Distribution,* 1st Edition (London: Oxford University Press, 1937), pp. 29-31.

[37] Margaret Hall, *Distributive Trading* (London: Hutchinson's University Library, 1949), p. 38.

[38] Julia Hood and B. S. Yamey, "Imperfect Competition in the Retail Trades," *Economica,* Vol. XVIII (1951), p. 136.

[39] Richard H. Holton, "Price Discrimination at Retail: The Supermarket Case," *The Journal of Industrial Economics,* Vol. VI, No. 1 (October, 1957), p. 28.

[40] Bob R. Holdren, *The Structure of a Retail Market and the Market Behavior of Retail Units* (Englewood Cliffs, New Jersey: Prentice-Hall, Inc., 1960), p. 182.

rivals. As we shall see, the supermarket is not overly addicted to price competition; price levels of competitors are watched closely, and, within given geographical market limits, competitors are generally quite few—all of which strongly suggests oligopolistic behavior.

Given the rather loose market structure which we have described, supermarkets, with their varied degree of firm and product differentiation, as well as spatial considerations which spring from the uniqueness of location, have some degree of monopoly power. One would thus conclude that individual supermarkets have negatively sloping demand, or average revenue curves, meaning that at higher prices the firm loses some but not all sales and that individual supermarket operators can exercise some discretion in determining price policies and price levels. Thus, theoretically, the firm should produce to the point where marginal cost equals marginal revenue—where the rate of change in total costs equals the rate of change in total receipts.

But, is this the case? The answer, of course, is indeterminate for a number of reasons. First, many operators have insufficient standards for maximizing their operations—they simply do not understand a maximizing model. Those who do grasp the concept of maximizing, given the nature of retail operations, think in terms of maximizing gross-margin dollars, a not too unrealistic assumption in the case of supermarkets. And, second, accounting costs are frequently inadequate for measuring or estimating the economic or opportunity costs of the firm's operations.

Food pricing by supermarkets, much the same as pricing for other commodities by other industries, is determined to a great extent by the relationships of supply and demand. The combined demand schedule for food, the basic products sold by supermarkets, is estimated to have a price elasticity of -.3 to -.4. The range for individual food items varies, largely between -.2 and -1.0.[41] This small range of elasticities means that retail grocery stores *in total* could not induce consumers to increase materially the total quantity

---

[41] Karl A. Fox, *The Analysis of Demand for Farm Products*, U.S. Department of Agriculture Technical Bulletin 1081 (Washington: U.S. Government Printing Office, 1953), p. 70.

of food consumed by any minor price changes. However, supermarket pricing policies are readily adapted to the various differences
in price elasticity for different commodities.[42]

Current Supermarket Pricing Policies

Supermarket pricing policies are formulated, in the main, within
the framework of the basic economic forces of supply and demand.
There are, however, several built-in institutional restraints which
affect this framework. A single supermarket operator cannot afford
the indulgence of severe price cuts for fear of the retaliatory actions
of his competitors; therefore, most supermarkets, because of the
uncertainty of demand reactions in both the immediate and long-
run future, are extremely hesitant to initiate drastic price-cutting
policies. For these reasons, most supermarket managers are content
to adjust their pricing policies to the most profitable level of operation under the prevailing local or regional rules of the game. In
most local and regional trading areas, there appears to exist a
rather well-defined and established "pecking order" among supermarkets as to who dares make the initial price cut and the extent
of the price reduction.

Price still continues to be an important and effective appeal
for most supermarkets, and the industry is still attempting to maintain the image and aura of a low-price retail institution. Many supermarket establishments today still find price appeals to be essential
to their over-all merchandising strategies. And these beliefs are
manifested in such present practices as dollar sales, price reductions,
multiple pricing, and leader merchandising in the attempt to build
and increase store traffic.

To a great extent, consumers also still view the supermarket
as a low-price institution. This viewpoint is perhaps further indication of the supermarket operator's success in devising his price

---

[42] Price elasticity of demand is defined as $E = \dfrac{\dfrac{\triangle q}{q}}{\dfrac{-\triangle p}{p}}$ where q is quantity taken and
p is the price charged and $\triangle q$ and $\triangle p$ are small changes in quantity and price.
When E is > 1, demand for a product is said to be elastic, that is, sensitive to price
changes, and when E is < 1, demand is inelastic or insensitive to price changes.

policies. However, in a nationwide survey among 1,069 housewives, price ranked fourth as a reason for choosing a specific supermarket. Convenience was ranked first, followed by courtesy and friendliness, and variety of merchandise.[43]

Progressive Grocer has also undertaken to discover what attracts customers to supermarkets. One of its studies concluded that customers are not necessarily bargain hunters. However, if the customer could save a few cents here and there, she was pleased. The study concluded that customers generally did not know prices, but that items bought week after week gave a pretty good clue to the price competitiveness of the store.[44]

The results of these studies appeared to show that price was not the primary reason that customers shopped particular supermarkets.

Supermarket Pricing Philosophy

Supermarket operators long ago abandoned the pricing strategy, still practiced today by many retail institutions, of marking up goods so as to maintain the same percentage markup on all goods. However, supermarkets do, with some exceptions, follow a practice of normal markups for particular lines, modifying the markup when competitive or other conditions warrant.[45] As an example, consider that a canned good costs 10¢ and the normal markup is 10 per cent based upon the selling price, then

$$\text{Retail price} = \frac{\text{cost}}{100\% - \text{markup \% at retail}} = \frac{10\cancel{\,c}}{(100\% - 10\%)} = 11\cancel{\,c}$$

thus the item would sell at 11¢ per can.

This price may be shaded in order to meet local competition, and, conversely, where local restraints might be overlooked, a slightly higher price may be charged. Apparently, the supermarket operator is interested in setting prices slightly lower on some commodities, taking normal markups on some lines, and taking higher

---

[43] See *The Housewife and the Food Industry* (New York: Kenyon and Eckhart, Inc., 1960), p. 8.

[44] "How Much Do Customers Know about Retail Prices," *Progressive Grocer* (February, 1964), pp. C104-C106.

[45] Holdren, *op. cit.*, pp. 73-88. Here Holdren discusses the decision process and the various markups used in pricing specific goods including cereals, bakery products, meats, poultry, fish, dairy products, fresh fruits and vegetables, and other supermarket commodities.

than normal markups on some items, reasoning that the balanced year-end effect will result in the greatest contribution to store profits. One argument frequently advanced is that the variations in supermarket margins for different classes of goods are based upon the operator's estimates of consumer demand functions. This may help explain the difference in pricing strategy for food as opposed to nonfood or general merchandise lines. General merchandise lines have, since their inception into supermarkets' product mix, characteristically carried a higher gross margin than the more conventional grocery items. The Colonial Study reports margins for classes of general merchandise lines ranging from 19.2 per cent for toys and games to 34.8 per cent for stationery.[46] One should recall that the over-all gross margin of supermarkets averages about 20 per cent. Obviously, something about the nature of general merchandise lines permits the taking of higher margins. Professor Bob R. Holdren approaches the variations in margins from this point of view.[47] His basic assumption is that shoppers seek to minimize the time and energy inputs expanded on grocery shopping. Price reductions on certain types of items are likely to persuade customers to visit particular stores. These price reductions may be on the items about which consumers are particularly price conscious—probably the ones purchased most frequently, and the ones which serve as the planning nuclei for shopping trips. In other words, these are the conventional grocery items: meats, potatoes, detergents, canned foods, and perhaps produce. Higher margins can be, and are, taken on the items which are not central to the consumer's decision to select one store or another. These may be the general merchandise lines such as health and beauty aids, hardware, and so forth.

Albert Ralphs of Ralphs Supermarkets, Inc., stated that Von's (Ralphs' arch and perennial rival) reduced margins across the board on general merchandise lines to levels approaching the normal over-all supermarket gross margin. Ralphs felt compelled to match these prices. Albert Ralphs' fear was that prices of these

---

[46] "The Colonial Study," *op. cit.,* p. C15.

[47] These ideas were imparted to this writer via personal interview with their originator during the summer of 1960 in Bloomington, Indiana. They appear, with further embellishments, in Holdren, *op. cit.,* pp. 67-100.

lines would be a long time in reaching previous levels, providing, that is, that they ever do.[48]

Generally speaking, however, supermarkets claim to use standard margins over invoice costs, and the standard margin is one that allows the supermarket to make a "satisfactory" profit and remain reasonably competitive. In other words, the supermarket operators claim to utilize average cost pricing.[49] Exact pricing margins are determined by the supermarket operator after carefully analyzing his competitors' pricing strategy and then by scrutinizing his cost of goods sold, indirect expenses, direct expenses, and administrative expenses, plus making some estimate as to the turnover or volume of sale for the items in question. The exact determination of each of these variables is an extremely difficult task. Problems of allocating costs are perhaps the biggest problems faced by the operator. Specific handling costs generally have little bearing on the determination of markup ratios. The large supermarket chains have never attempted to make extensive studies of the distribution costs allocable to individual items or classes of items.

The simple truth is that many supermarket operators do not know the relative handling and selling costs attached to the various items sold in their stores. In spite of this limitation, the supermarket operator must nonetheless make appraisals of these factors, and these costs are imputed in determining the markup of many of his commodities.

The Use of Leader Pricing Policies

In an attempt to increase over-all store profits, some supermarket operators follow a practice known as leader pricing.[50] Leader merchandise pricing frequently is explained in a number of ways. The practice is most often defined as knowingly and intentionally marking a part of the stock at prices that will not yield the greatest dollar profit return on these particular goods. The articles that are

[48] Personal interview with Albert Ralphs of Ralphs Supermarkets, Inc., Los Angeles, California, Winter, 1961.
[49] Holdren, *op. cit.,* p. 73.
[50] This practice is nearly ubiquitous in the supermarket field. During the author's personal interviewing with 20 executives in the supermarket and the food field, the question, "Do you believe in and practice leader pricing?" was asked. All agreed they did, and many commented that this was perhaps one of the supermarket industry's most effective pricing techniques.

then selected for special price emphasis are identified as "leaders." Loss leader pricing is the practice of marking goods for sale with a retail price that does not cover costs.[51] Loss leader pricing is construed by many states as being an unfair method of competition, and sales of this type are prohibited by Unfair Sales Practices Acts. These acts generally prescribe the minimum markup above cost on merchandise sold. This type of legislation is difficult to enforce but does provide some damper on price cutting in the form of loss leaders.

However, because of the many ambiguities within these "Unfair Trade Practices Acts" or "Unfair Sales Acts," and the difficulties inherent in policing and enforcing this legislation, many supermarkets practice "loss leader" as well as "leader" merchandise pricing policies.

As was mentioned earlier, general price cuts as a competitive tool of supermarkets are seldom employed for fear of retaliation of competition and other reasons. However, the use of price specials or leaders as a promotional device appears to create less disturbance among competition. This is largely due to the fact that price specials or leaders are considered normal rules of the game, and they often result not just from price-cutting decisions by the supermarket, but also from price cutting and special discounts granted by manufacturers and other suppliers.

Leader pricing is widely used in the belief that the practice pulls customers into the store, thus increasing store traffic and exposing more customers to a greater number of conventional and higher-markup impulse items. Leader merchandise pricing is further used to create the general impression of over-all low prices. Because the total number of items within the average supermarket may number as many as 7,000, the customer cannot possibly be familiar with more than a few prices. Consequently, leader prices must be placed on high-frequency traffic items. Examples of effective "leaders" are such items as meat, detergents, and coffee.[52]

---

[51] Costs may be construed to be cost of goods sold, or cost of goods sold plus some "normal" markup percentage.

[52] Holdren, *op. cit.*, p. 73.

Other Supermarket Pricing Practices

Many supermarket operators have embraced the pricing policy of using "odd" as opposed to "even" number figures, in the belief that there exists a certain psychological advantage to the odd numbers. In the food store advertisements included in one study, by far the most popular prices were 29 cents, 39 cents, and 49 cents. As a matter of fact, 57 per cent of the entire 2,597 prices ended in "9" while in second place was "5," with 15 per cent.[53]

From the predominance of odd prices, it would appear that retailers believe they have advantages over even prices. It is often claimed that a 19-cent price may move many more units of an article than a 20-cent price, simply because people believe that they are getting a bargain, the odd price being a sign that the price has been cut as far as possible. However, odd vs. even price endings today probably result more from custom than from astute use of psychology.

Another pricing and merchandising technique gaining increasing attention from supermarket operators is multiple-unit pricing. Much impetus has been given to multiple-unit pricing by manufacturers who package items in multiple units. The attempt made is to increase the unit sale of these commodities by either a real or psychological savings appeal to the customer. The multiple-unit package is generally priced a few cents below the total price of the individual items.

A Look Ahead

The establishment of supermarket pricing policies and techniques remains more an art than a science. The complicated and intricate number of variables and their interactions are all but too much for the supermarket operator to control. Imperfections in the market mechanism, plus the imperfections in the price setter's own knowledge, force him to rely heavily on his experience and merchandising skill, plus his intuitive knowledge of the pricing situation. There are few "pat" formulas which will enable the operator to choose the right price on any given occasion. Pricing strategy must remain

---

[53] D. W. Twedt, "Does the '9 Fixation' in Retail Pricing Really Promote Sales?" *Journal of Marketing*, Vol. XXIX, No. 4 (October, 1964), p. 55.

a highly individualized concept for each store. Great variations will exist in pricing policies among various stores, and new competitors are already causing many supermarket operators to reevaluate existing pricing policies and techniques. The food discount houses and omnibus discount stores have learned that food, cheaply priced, is a strong stimulant to customer traffic.

One operator stated that possibly supermarkets might counter the inroads of discount competition by going overwhelmingly to the massive use of leaders. Instead of the super featuring only 15 to 20 items as leaders, perhaps 100 or so items would be featured, at unusually low prices, in an effort to create the discount and bargain atmosphere.[54]

Some food operators are attempting to bolster their competitive positions by the use of bank-credit charge plans for their supermarket sales. If credit selling should become widely adopted in this form, or should the retailer be forced to carry his own accounts, the result may be drastically altered supermarket price policies. The consensus of most supermarket operators is that neither they nor the customers are anxious to see widespread credit selling return to food retailing.[55] Given the increased incidence of bank credit cards, it is likely, however, that more and more supermarkets will offer this credit service, especially to their higher-income clientele who can qualify for such cards.

In the future, as in the past, supermarket pricing policies will remain an important and viable part of the supermarkets' total merchandising strategy.

Trends in Supermarket Promotion Policies

The scope and importance of supermarket promotional activities are seldom realized either by the individual store or by all the stores taken together as an industry. Actual figures are difficult to obtain, but some indication of the financial magnitude of promotional activities is as follows: All supermarkets spend somewhere in the

---

[54] Interview with Marsh Blackburn, Owner-manager, Hoosier Brokerage Co., Indianapolis, Indiana, Summer, 1961.

[55] This conclusion was reached after examining many articles in the trade literature and, further, through discussions with several top management people in the food field.

neighborhood of $1,261 million a year for advertising and promotional activities. This figure means that each supermarket on the average spends slightly more than $38,000 per year for promotional activities, or about 2.5 per cent of total sales.[56]

In the conventional parlance of the economist, promotional activities are those that attempt to alter or influence shifts in the firm's demand curve. Although additional types may sometimes be used, promotional activities normally fall into three distinct categories: (1) advertising, (2) personal selling, and (3) special in-store displays.[57]

Primary emphasis of this section will be on developments in advertising, or what are called out-of-store promotions and in-store promotional activities such as mass displays, point-of-purchase materials, contests, premium plans, and trading stamps. Certainly the two forms are frequently combined for greater emphasis, such as a newspaper ad featuring a particular article plus an in-store mass display of this article. Trading stamps are another example of a promotional activity that is both outside the store; *i.e.,* newspaper ad featuring and promoting a stamp plan, and in-store check-out personnel pushing stamps and other in-store stamp displays.

Newspaper Advertising

Advertising is any paid nonpersonal presentation of goods, ideas, or services.[58] For the supermarket, advertising means primarily the use of newspapers, radio, handbills and circulars, and television. Newspaper advertising continues to be the most important advertising medium for supermarkets. The Super Market Institute reports that 96 per cent of its members used newspaper advertising in 1966, 69 per cent used handbills and circulars, 59 per cent used radio, and 28 per cent used television.[59] When this writer presented an arrayed

---

[56] This figure was obtained in the following manner: The Super Market Institute figure exchange lists 2.5 per cent as the average expenditure by supermarkets for advertising and promotion. Applying this percentage to the total volume of supermarkets (both chain and independent) for 1966, we get $1,261 million. This figure divided by total number of supermarkets (32,705) equals $38,000 plus.

[57] John A. Howard, *Marketing Management: Analysis and Decision* (Homewood, Illinois: Richard D. Irwin, Inc., 1963), p. 387.

[58] Delbert J. Duncan and Charles F. Phillips, *Retailing Principles and Methods* (Homewood, Illinois: Richard D. Irwin, Inc., 1967), p. 519.

[59] *The Super Market Industry Speaks, op. cit.*

list of 13 promotional devices known to be used by supermarkets
to 20 food and supermarket executives and asked them to choose
what they considered to be the most important promotional tool for
their operation, the overwhelming choice was newspaper advertising. The reasons for this are apparent. From the consumers' point
of view, the newspaper is a valuable means of comparing and con-
trasting item prices, a particularly important practice in the food
goods category. Of the households in the United States, 87 per cent
are reached by the circulation of the newspaper.[60]

Because of the tendency of customers to do most of their purchasing on Thursdays, Fridays, and Saturdays, supermarkets run the
bulk of their newspaper advertising on Wednesdays.[61] These advertisements are known in the trade as "the weekly food ads." The
Super Market Institute reports that 63 per cent of their total
members' advertising is placed in Wednesday's paper.[62] This means
that the individual super advertisement must be read and compared
with whatever advertising from competition might appear.

In an effort to change customer shopping habits and smooth
out the weekly sales, many supermarkets are experimenting with
early-week newspaper advertising. These efforts are being met with
mixed success. Monday and Tuesday combined account for only
36 per cent of the total week's advertising.[63] Many stores are
experimenting with institutional advertisements in newspapers on
week ends and early in the week. These institutional advertisements
attempt to build up the store's reputation and prestige in the eyes
of the customers. Frequent themes are quality of merchandise,
reputation of the company, convenience of the store's offerings, and
constant low prices. In essence, the stores are attempting to build
favorable customer images.[64] In light of the perennial criticism
of supermarket newspaper advertising, that food ads are dull, un-
informative, and unimaginative, this would appear to be a commendable effort. One writer commented as follows: "Food ad-

[60] Bureau of Advertising, American Newspaper Publishers Association Inc., 1965,
in Otto Kleppner, *Advertising Procedure,* 5th ed. (Englewood Cliffs, New Jersey:
Prentice-Hall, Inc., 1966), p. 179.
[61] *The Super Market Industry Speaks, op. cit.,* p. 20.
[62] *Ibid.*
[63] *Ibid.*
[64] "New Image Plus Price Appeal," *Chain Store Age* (June, 1965), p. 68.

vertising is the most thoroughly criticized advertising in the world."[65] Many supermarket operators are making valiant efforts to overcome these criticisms.

In the larger chain organizations, sales promotion managers are being instructed to supervise individual store's advertising and promotional efforts. Trained artists and layout experts are being employed to do a better job of creating advertisements. Many of the smaller stores and independents are getting more and better help from the headquarters of voluntary and cooperative organizations. Greater attention is being placed on the selection of the items, size of advertisement, art work, and other factors. Some operators, in a bid to gain increased customer acceptance and appeal in their food advertisements, are moving rapidly to the use of color in newspapers.

Others, in an effort to increase the effectiveness of their newspaper advertisements, are going to the dramatic use of illustration, increased white space, variety of type sizes, and humorous cartoons. Newspapers, in spite of some shortcomings, are likely to remain the most important advertising medium for supermarkets.

The strength of newspaper advertising in relation to other media is attested to by the fact that nearly 90 per cent of the members of the Super Market Institute spend more for newspaper advertising than in any other medium; 82 per cent spend more on newspapers than in all other media combined.[66]

Furthermore, the effectiveness of newspapers can be attributed to their availability at the time of decision and purchase and the believability of their factual reporting. This, in turn, makes newspapers appropriate for reporting information about new products, for telling about current availability and sales, where to get things, and the actual prices of products. The aim of most newspaper advertising focuses on how to do things to satisfy the desires one already has. A limitation of the medium is that because there are so few newspapers with such widespread daily consumption, it lacks

[65] William J. Quinn, "Advertising in Action," Summary Report NAFC Management Clinic, *Sales Promotion and Advertising,* January, 1955, p. 42.

[66] *The Super Market Industry Speaks, op. cit.,* p. 20.

uniqueness. It is perceived as a mass medium with little indi-
viduality.[67]

Radio

Radio is not generally considered the primary advertising medium of supermarkets. As was previously stated, 59 per cent of the
members of the Super Market Institute reportedly used some radio
in their promotional activity.

Food retailers differ markedly in their opinions on the effectiveness of radio advertising. One study—although somewhat dated—
indicated that radio is considered ideal for promoting mass-consumer
goods of low unit price whose sale may be motivated by the use
of emotional appeals. Such supermarket items as food, drugs, soaps,
and detergents fit well into the emotional-appeal category.[68] "While
the radio does not seem to be particularly well fitted for retail
advertising, it can be used with some effectiveness, evidently, for
the publicizing of retail institutions which feature low price merchandise, even of a durable type; or which stress easy payment, and
can be used even to some degree to promote a limited number of
specific items of merchandise."[69] Inasmuch as supermarket advertising is frequently based on a price appeal, radio becomes less
effective because of the difficulty of injecting emotional appeals
into price advertising.

However, radio does lend itself quite well to supermarket advertising in a number of respects. Radio is quite an adaptable and
flexible medium. The advertising message can be changed readily
without undue delays or lead time. Radio is especially effective for
"plugging" special in-store promotions and for institutional spot
announcements.

Nevertheless, the character of radio has changed remarkably
during the last several years, and these changes are causing many
advertisers to reappraise their plans so as to include less radio. One
supermarket executive commented:

---

[67] Harper Boyd and Sidney J. Levy, *Promotion: A Behavioral View* (Englewood
Cliffs, New Jersey: Prentice-Hall, Inc., 1967), p. 89.
[68] R. Cassady, Jr., and R. M. Williams, "Radio As An Advertising Medium,"
Harvard Business Review, January, 1949, p. 62.
[69] *Ibid.*

Since the advent of television and the disintegration of network radio, radio stations are nothing more than broadcasters of news and music. It's my belief that only adolescents listen to most of the local stations and that isn't our market.[70]

However, radio in conjunction with other media will undoubtedly remain an important and integral part of the supermarket's sales promotion activity. For instance, radio and newspapers work very well as complementary media for reaching customers. And in the competitive scramble for new business, the supermarket operator cannot afford to overlook the sales ability of effective radio advertising.

Television

Television advertising has been looked upon by many supermarket operators with a great deal of trepidation. The newness alone of the medium has caused many to adopt an attitude of "wait and see." Television advertising can be a most expensive form of supermarket promotion. A supermarket's trading area is hardly ever as large as, nor does the area necessarily coincide with, the telecasting area of the television station. Thus, the advertiser is frequently paying for much waste circulation. For this reason, the independent supermarket operator has avoided the extensive use of television advertising. However, for the chain supermarket or independent which belongs to a voluntary chain organization, television advertising can be used much more effectively.[71]

Trends appear to indicate that television advertising is growing in importance for supermarket operators, especially those belonging to chain organizations which can spread the cost of a syndicated program or series of spot commercials over a large number of stores. However, several limitations of television as an advertising medium are reported by Settel:[72]

1. Multiple item advertising on television is too difficult.
2. TV best lends itself to institutional advertising and institutional advertising cannot be evaluated effectively.

---

[70] Personal interview—respondent wished to remain anonymous.
[71] "Five Ways Stores Are Combating New Competition," *Chain Store Age,* May, 1965, p. 68.
[72] Irving Settel, "Why Retailers Bypass Television," *Journal of Retailing,* Winter, 1955-56, p. 181.

3. Most desirable time periods on television are not available to retailers.

4. Too much planning and time is involved to produce effective programs and commercials.

5. Local shows produced by retailers cannot compete with network shows.

6. Other forms of advertising—radio and newspaper—offer more to the retailer than does television.

7. Newspapers reach the largest audience for every advertising dollar spent.

8. Most food store operators consider the cost of television too high and feel the money spent cannot produce as many customers as newspaper, direct mail, and radio advertising.

Handbills and Direct Mail

For the smaller independent supermarket operator, and for that matter even some large national chains, handbills and direct mail circulars are rapidly becoming the second most important medium for advertising. Handbills and direct mail circulars appear to possess almost the ideal combination of qualities sought by supermarket operators in choosing a medium.

First of all, the cost of direct mail or handbills can be tailored readily to the desired amount of expenditure by the supermarket. And, secondly, the supermarket can advertise, via circulars or direct mail, directly in the trading area which surrounds the store. Waste circulation is thus largely eliminated.

Rather astounding results are being reported, stemming from supers' use of circulars and handbills,[73] but as in the use of all media, the effectiveness depends upon the strength of the appeal, the choice of items, quality of production, and other factors. During the last few years, handbills and circulars have replaced radio as the second most important medium for advertising and promotion.

In-Store Promotional Activities

There are a variety of types of in-store supermarket promotional activities. Those that are more prominently engaged in are in-store displays, premiums, contests, and trading stamps.

Special Displays. The logic and success of special displays are

[73] "Handbill Advertising Brings 11% Volume Gain," *Progressive Grocer*, January, 1960, p. 119.

predicated on two factors. One, and perhaps most important, is that supermarkets are self-service stores. The customers are encouraged to shop the aisles, cases, and gondolas for items of their choice. Second, the rate or incidence of impulse buying is extremely high. Therefore, given these two factors—self-service merchandise and a high rate of impulse purchasing—the natural effect would appear to be a strong stimulus to the store operator to use a large number of special displays.

The effectiveness of special display has long been evident. One study reports that 5 per cent of the total supermarket sales are the result of special displays.[74] Special displays take the form of end displays, slot displays, mass displays, and small displays of both food and general merchandise items.

There are many reasons why supermarkets are using more special displays. Several of these reasons are:

1. Probably foremost is the desire to increase store sales and profits.
2. To increase sales of related line products.
3. For decorative purposes; enhance appearance of store.
4. To create a buying psychology on part of customer through psychological techniques of mass, color, and arrangement.
5. To create a "price" atmosphere.
6. To stimulate impulse buying.
7. To alter or influence customer traffic patterns.
8. To move out dead or slow-moving merchandise.

A modern-day testimonial as to the effectiveness of special displays in increasing a store's sales is the Dillon Study. The results of this study (highlights of which are presented in Table 4.4) showed that the average special display boosts sales 536 per cent over normal shelf-position movement.[75]

This study appears as rather pointed evidence of the effect of additional display opportunities. In addition to using just more displays, the operator must understand and use to his advantage the technique of making special displays more effective.

Dr. Ernest Dichter, President of the Institute for Research in Mass Motivations, Inc., has stated that " . . . . Displays must sell the customer immediately because the customer is not in a reason-

---

[74] See, "Improving Sale Item Display: The Display and Merchandising Workshop," *Chain Store Age*, January, 1965, p. 64.

[75] "The Dillon Study," *Progressive Grocer*, October, 1960, p. D81.

TABLE 4.4

RESULTS OF DILLON STUDY 16-WEEK SPECIAL DISPLAY AUDIT

	1st Period before Special Display	*2nd Period after Special Display*	*Per Cent Change*
Total Number Items Displayed	360	507	+40.8
Total Display Exposures	734	1,169	+59.2
Display Dollar Sales Per Cent of Total Grocery Sales	5	8	+60.0
Display Dollar Margin Per Cent of Total Grocery Margin	5	7	+40.0
Display Average Weekly Dollar Sales per Store	$1,000	$1,782	+78.2
Display Average Weekly Dollar Margin per Store	$ 177	$ 288	+62.7
Display Average Weekly Unit Sales per Store	3,420	6,767	+97.8

Source: "The Dillon Study," *Progressive Grocer,* October, 1960, p. D81.

ing mood. All the customer can do is react emotionally and quickly, and you have either made your point or not."[76] Dichter reasons that there are three prime purposes of displays and that to recognize these is to make your display more effective:[77]

1. To climax the conditioned reflex of advertising, where such advertising has been proved effective in making up the consumer's mind.
2. To break the conditioned reflex when another product may have had more or equal effectiveness in influencing the buying public.

And when one is dealing with new products or the objective is to stimulate a latent desire to splurge, there is a third objective:

3. Why not? . . . . Why not try something you have never tried before? Why not pamper yourself? Why not get a luxury item you did not dare buy until now?

Undoubtedly, much research remains to be done in terms of analyzing and evaluating the effectiveness of various techniques of displaying merchandise. Most merchants are uncertain about what will happen to the sales volume of an entire department if the

[76] Ernest Dichter, "The Point of Point of Purchase," *Food Marketing,* May-June, 1954, p. 1.
[77] *Ibid.*

display space is increased or decreased, or if the location of the display within the store is changed. Aside from a few limited studies in the grocery field, the problem has seen little orderly investigation.[78] One researcher in this area, commenting on the need for further study in this area, stated the following:

> Just as items vary in their price elasticity of demand, they also vary in their display elasticity of demand. Since the retailer may have more control over the display policy with his store than he does over the prices placed on certain classes of items, this would appear to be a highly profitable area for careful study.[79]

Because of the inherent features of its operation, the supermarket offers one of the greatest opportunities in the retail field to capitalize on the psychological displaying of products.

Premiums. Supermarkets have long used premiums as a means of increasing store traffic, developing customer patronage, and, of course, increasing store profits. However, premium promotion is not without its problems for the supermarket operators. Most premium promotions are undertaken as a result of manufacturer initiative rather than the initiative of the individual store. One trade association spokesman said that many stores are beginning to rebel against the practice of acting as clearing houses for manufacturers' premiums. "The time and expense to the supermarket operator is just too great, and unless the manufacturers can find ways of overcoming these problems, premiums (manufacturers) will just have to go."[80]

Trading Stamps. Feelings about trading stamps seem to fall decidedly into two categories: those violently opposing the use of stamps and those staunchly defending their use. Two well-known and recognized authorities on the use and practices of trading stamps wrote the following characterization, which seems to describe this controversial promotional device:

---

[78] For example see U.S. Department of Agriculture, Production and Marketing Administration, Marketing Research Report No. 30, *Better Allocation of Selling Space in Food Stores: Part I—Relation of Size of Display to Sales of Canned Fruits and Vegetables* (Washington: U.S. Government Printing Office, November, 1952), and *The Super Value Study* (New York: *Progressive Grocer,* 1958).

[79] Edgar A. Pessemier, "Applying Supermarket Techniques to Non-food Retailing," *Journal of Retailing,* Summer, 1960, p. 110.

[80] Personal interview—respondent desired to remain anonymous.

In the history of American business no single promotional device since the advent of mass advertising in the early part of the
century appears to have attracted so much attention—favorable and
otherwise—as trading stamps in recent years. For the first 60 years
of their gradually increasing use by aggressive merchants as a device
for attracting new customers and holding the trade of old customers,
stamps received only sporadic public notice. When the supermarkets
began, about five years ago, to offer trading stamps as an added
inducement to customers in highly competitive situations, stamps
became, almost overnight, one of the most controversial subjects on
the American scene.[81]

The task here is not to analyze and evaluate the controversial nature of trading stamps. Rather, the purpose is to survey the major
trends in the use of trading stamps today. Perhaps of paramount importance to the use of trading stamps is customer acceptance. And
the American housewife is noted for her affinity for stamps.

In light of this strong customer acceptance, supermarkets continue to use stamps as a strong promotional device. The Super
Market Institute reports that a survey of its members for 1966
shows that stamps declined slightly in importance as a promotional
device.

In 1966, trading stamps were given in 61 per cent of the
supermarkets, the smallest proportion since 1959. Some 48 per cent
of the companies now offer stamps to their customers, compared
with 51 per cent a year ago. This marks the first time since 1959
that fewer than half of the companies are giving stamps. Regionally,
a majority of the supermarkets issue trading stamps in every region
except New England and the East North Central—led by the West
South Central region, where stamps are given in fully 88 per cent
of the supermarkets.[82]

Multiple-stamp days were reported for 18 per cent of the
supermarkets which give stamps, and in 90 per cent of these
supers, multiple stamps are offered regularly one day a week.[83]

Progressive Grocer, whose annual report samples a somewhat
different-sized group of supermarkets, reports that in 1966 there
was a very slight decrease in the per cent of supermarkets giving

---

[81] Albert Haring and Wallace O. Yoder (eds.), *Trading Stamp Practice and Pricing
Policy* (Bloomington, Indiana: Bureau of Business Research, School of Business,
Indiana University, 1958), p. 299.
[82] *The Super Market Industry Speaks, op. cit.,* p. 22.
[83] *Ibid.*

stamps, and at year's end approximately 42 per cent of independent supermarkets and over 60 per cent of chain supermarkets were offering trading stamps.[84]

What about consumer reactions? Many independents have actively and aggressively engaged in anti-stamp campaigns in an attempt to discourage customers from saving stamps. And as more and more food stores in a neighborhood continue to offer stamps, does the consumer lose interest in saving them as many food retailers feared she would? The answers to this and many other questions were recently given in a study entitled "Can Attitude Measurement Predict Consumer Behavior?" The general consensus of this study is that the customer still likes stamps—not because she thinks she is getting something for nothing when she receives and pastes stamps. But she still thinks what she is getting is of value. The stamps she saves—whether green, gold, blue, or plaid—can still be a powerful attraction to pulling her back into the doors of a stamp-giving supermarket.[85]

However, there appears to be increasing evidence that food merchants are definitely becoming more and more disenchanted with stamps and that housewives, especially the higher-income and better-informed purchasers, are, too, becoming somewhat disaffected with saving stamps. The trend away from stamps is noticeable among both chains and independents. The decline in stamp popularity does not seem to be appreciably caused or affected by consumer price protests, which are more often directed at games and contests, as opposed to stamps. The discontinuance of stamps in many stores appears according to plan and as a manifestation of retailer recognition of the growing appeal of price, as compared with stamps which no longer carry their earlier import.[86]

Contests. Contests have become of such magnitude that, except for very large operations, the contest design, rules, procedures, judg-

---

[84] Thirty-Fourth Annual Report of the Grocery Industry, *Progressive Grocer,* April, 1967, p. 66.

[85] Jon G. Udell, "Can Attitude Measurement Predict Consumer Behavior?" *Journal of Marketing,* Vol. 29, October, 1965, pp. 46-50.

[86] For a comprehensive discussion of the use and future of trading stamps in food stores, see "Organization and Competition in Food Retailing," Technical Study No. 7, *Report of the National Commission on Food Marketing,* U.S. Government Printing Office, June, 1966, pp. 437-475.

ing, etc. are turned over to a special contest company. Of course, many smaller local and regional contests are still undertaken by the supermarket organization itself. A contest is a promotion device and must therefore accomplish a promotional goal, *i.e.,* increase traffic, sales, or profits, in order to justify the contest.

Currently, one of the most accepted contests is one that requires the entrants to do nothing but sign their names and leave the rest to fate. Food supermarkets are finding this type of contest to be an effective promotion.[87]

As operator interest in trading stamps declines, it is quite likely that there will be an accelerated interest in games and contests as substitute promotional devices. An interesting and not too unusual phenomenon is the recent tendency for games and contests in supermarkets to spread to gasoline service stations and vice versa. One of the latest games on the scene is called "Double Sweepstakes Bingo." The game is aimed at catching the American housewife at both her supermarket and gas station. Most of the popular consumer games involve a variation on conventional bingo, the matching of halves of cards or scenes, or the completion of words. The cash prizes range from $1.00 to $2,500, with $1,000 being the average top prize. Many supermarket operators, however, report that following the boycotts in the fall of 1966, some consumers are becoming increasingly angry over food store prices. In view of this reaction, some members of the industry are trying to get away from games and go to discount pricing as a sales stimulus.

Changing Attitudes Regarding Supermarket Promotional Policies

The supermarket operator, faced with shrinking margins and rising expenses, is becoming ever more concerned with getting full value from his promotional dollar. The supermarket operator can no longer afford to promote for the "sake of promoting," but instead must choose his promotional mix, his media, and his promotional appeals, with an eye toward increased volume of business and better profits. Most firms seem to feel that there are advantages to using multiple media. However, the nucleus of this package is becoming ever more frequently the newspaper.

---

[87] "Do Games Pay Off?" *Super Market News,* June 21, 1965, p. 32.

Many supermarkets are rapidly turning away from simple food advertisements or promotions. A marked improvement in supermarket advertising is the promotion of a theme. This trend results in supermarkets selling and promoting meals, conveniences, time savers, and a way of life.[88]

In-store displays, contests, and premiums continue to play an important part as supermarket promotional devices. However, the key to success for supermarket premiums and contests is simplicity. Owners are becoming dissatisfied with many practices of manufacturers and suppliers which load the store manager with administrative burdens and responsibilities and actually do little to promote the individual store and its products.

Trading stamps are beginning to decline in importance as a supermarket promotional device. But in spite of some adverse legislation and increased resistance from some independent operators, customers continue saving stamps and patronizing stores which offer them.

Trends in Buying Policies and Decisions

Much of what would normally be considered as part of a supermarket's buying policy or policies, *i.e.,* influx of new products, private vs. national brands, and stocking of nonfoods, has been discussed in previous sections of this chapter. Certain areas remain, however, which warrant some comment and elaboration in regard to supermarket buying policies and decisions. Buying policies are an integral and important part of a supermarket's total merchandising strategy.

Supermarkets in 1966 sold $50.45 billion worth of food and general merchandise items.[89] When one considers that approximately 80 per cent of these sales represent cost of goods, the magnitude of supermarket purchases can be seen. Supermarkets in 1966 bought merchandise resources totalling nearly $41 billion. These figures perhaps explain why manufacturers and suppliers go to such lengths to win favor with supermarket buyers.

---

[88] "Promote the Whole Store," *Food Merchandising,* April, 1960, p. 26.
[89] Thirty-Fourth Annual Report of the Grocery Industry, *op. cit.,* p. 62.

The following issues, as they affect a firm's buying policies and decisions, will be discussed:

1. Buying arrangements for chain supermarket organizations.
2. Buying committees.
3. Use of buying associations.
4. Source of supply for general merchandise items.
5. Make or buy decisions.

Buying Arrangements of Chain Supermarket Organizations

Because of the variety of sizes of independent supers, and the personal predilections of managers, a number of different buying arrangements for independents, as opposed to chain organizations, are likely to evolve. Certainly the independent supermarket owner/manager must ultimately take the responsibility of buying the merchandise for his store. When the owner/manager is blessed with capable department managers and assistants, he may delegate responsibility for buying particular merchandise lines to various department or assistant managers. Independent supermarket operators, much like their chain competitors, may seek merchandise from manufacturers or resellers such as wholesalers, brokers, or rack jobbers. Although burdened by size limitations, the independent may also decide to manufacture some of his own commodities, for instance bread, cakes, or pastry items.

Chain organizations typically employ one of three types of institutionalized buying arrangements:[90]

1. Central merchandising. Here, planning, buying, pricing, and controlling stock are done centrally, with stores simply selling what they are sent.
2. Central purchase with store requisitions. Under this arrangement central buyers purchase and warehouse stocks, and store managers requisition goods as they need them. Sometimes the centrally purchased goods are held by the manufacturer for drop shipment to the store.
3. Price agreement plan. Under this arrangement central buyers decide what items stores may buy and the prices and terms of purchase, but the determination as to how much and when to buy is left to the stores. With all these variations there is an over-all organization with divisions for merchandising, store operations, and control.

---

[90] John W. Wingate, *Buying for Retail Stores* (New York: Prentice-Hall, Inc., 1956), p. 77. See also, Edgar A. Pessemier, "Division Organization in Food Chains," *Journal of Retailing,* Winter, 1957-1958, pp. 170-182.

Each of these arrangements is subject to advantages and disadvantages. Perhaps as many as 80 to 85 per cent of the items carried by, or purchased by, the supermarket are routine items such as canned goods, meats, produce, and dry groceries which call for standardized order procedures and central merchandising. Usually great cost economies can be secured for the chain organization under this arrangement. However, even with routine purchases, the buyer must be aware of special promotions, discounts, speed of delivery, and other special purchasing arrangements offered by suppliers. The greatest disadvantage to central purchasing is the lack of flexibility which may prohibit the store buyer from taking advantage of special conditions. With constantly increasing pressures of local competition, the supermarket operator must be always ready to adapt to local market situations. Therefore, a purchasing arrangement such as the Price Agreement Plan may make for a better strategic arrangement than the more rigid alternatives of strict centralized purchasing.

Many of the routine buying decisions involving such issues as economical handling, reorder points, quantities to purchase, and warehousing are being made with the help of computers and other electronic devices. Problems of out-of-stock, especially, have been minimized with the aid of these devices.[91]

A vast amount of integration has been undertaken by the supermarket industry. One source reported that 80 per cent of the supermarkets obtain their grocery products through their own central warehouses, from 9 to 10 per cent obtain their merchandise through retailer-owned cooperatives, 3 per cent through voluntary chain wholesalers, and 7 per cent through no central warehouse or affiliation.[92]

This large amount of integration for chains and the voluntary and cooperative activities of the independents have led to two important developments in supermarkets which affect the buying policies and procedures of the stores. These are: buying committees and the buying association. Each will be discussed in turn.

---

[91] "Data Processing," *Supermarket News,* October 18, 1965, pp. 58-60.
[92] See "Organization and Competition in Food Retailing," *op. cit.,* pp. 59-75.

Buying Committee. The buying committee is one widely employed method that chain supermarkets use to combat or adjust to the tremendous influx of new items available and suitable for supermarket merchandising. Each year countless thousands of new items are offered to supermarkets for sale. The decisions of the buying group for the chain as to whether to accept or reject new items are extremely important and, of course, the question of the chain's success or failure can hang in the balance.

The purpose of the buying committee is to:[93]

1. Remove buying decisions from an emotional atmosphere.
2. Prevent a buyer's personal likes and dislikes from entering into a decision.
3. Help store and field personnel better to understand buying operations at headquarters, through rotating participation of some members.
4. Capitalize on collective knowledge.
5. Provide for the orderly continuity of buying operations.

The essential question now becomes: "How well has the buying committee worked in practice?" The answer, though opinions do vary: "Not very well." And this is especially true as regards statements 1 and 2.

In the course of gathering research materials for this study, this writer interviewed 10 executives of food supermarket chains. Some of the largest chains in the country were included, as well as several smaller organizations. The general consensus about buying committees is about as follows: Two heads are better than one but there is nothing magical about using a committee. The committee is subjected to the same emotional forces as an individual buyer. In fact, some committees are a tremendous hazard if dominated by a strong individual. Here the members may just rubber stamp any decision made by the stronger person.

Other arguments are also being advanced against the over-enthusiastic use of buying committees. Some argue that a single individual must ultimately have both the authority and responsibility for making buying decisions. Committees are said to be excellent devices for building sound communications within the organization,

---

[93] Frank J. Charvat, *Supermarketing* (New York: The Macmillan Co., 1961), p. 78.

but are managerially weak because of divided or shared responsibilities.

Another argument, not necessarily to the detriment of the buying committee, is that, if as much concerted effort were devoted to selling or pushing items out of the supermarket as is devoted to keeping them out via buying restrictions, then buying committees could be much more lax in their vigilance and profits would likely improve.[94] However, until some new device or technique becomes available that represents some improvement, buying committees will undoubtedly continue to dominate supermarket chain buying policies and decisions.

Buying Associations. The size advantage of many large supermarket chains and the amount of integration undertaken have in many instances given these firms decided buying advantages over smaller independent competitors. However, the independent has attempted with much success to combat the buying and merchandising effectiveness of the large chains by associating with, or forming, either a voluntary or a cooperative chain.

In 1966, there were 77,000 food stores which were members of either voluntary chains, or cooperative organizations.[95] The distinction between these two forms is that voluntary groups are wholesaler sponsored and the cooperative group is retailer sponsored.

Admittedly, many of these food stores belonging to voluntary and cooperative organizations do not meet the volume requirements to be called supermarkets. On the other hand, many of them do, and these organizational arrangements offer a good opportunity for the smaller stores to gain some of the scale advantages and economies of their larger competitors. When an independent affiliates with either a voluntary or cooperative organization, many of his buying decisions are either eliminated or simplified via routinization. Many operators will authorize the wholesaler (either voluntary or cooperative) to ship many items on an automatic basis.[96] Thus, the store manager's time is freed to engage in more pressing merchandising activities.

---

[94] "Emphasis Shifts to the Selling Committees," *Progressive Grocer,* June, 1959, p. 6.
[95] Thirty-Fourth Annual Report of the Grocery Industry, *op. cit.,* p. 170.
[96] "Wholesale Success: Incentive Plus Service Adds Up to Profits for Voluntary Food Merchants," *Barron's,* 46:11t, July 4, 1966.

Buying General Merchandise Lines

The main or conventional sources of supply for food items in supermarkets are: (1) direct from manufacturers, (2) wholesalers, and (3) brokers. Because of the newness and vastness of general merchandise or nonfood lines and the unfamiliarity of most supermarket buyers with them, an important new source of supply and, consequently, new buying techniques have come about for this important product group.

The rack jobber is this new supplier, and his operation works essentially in this manner: He buys the merchandise at wholesale prices, adds his markup and the store's and usually puts the retail price tag on each item. As new merchandise is added to the racks, the store is billed. If the merchandise does not sell within a certain period, the jobber takes the merchandise away and credits the grocer for that amount.[97] In many instances, a single supermarket may be serviced by as many as 10 or 12 rack jobbers specializing in the sale of such products as health and beauty aids, housewares, hardware, toys, stationery, records, and soft goods.

The decision to use rack jobbers and the extent of their use will differ, of course, from supermarket organization to organization. Even within the same chain one division may choose to rely heavily on rack jobbers while another division, because it may possess more specialized skills in general merchandise lines, may go to a more direct source of supply.

The importance of rack jobbers as a source of supply will vary widely according to product lines. Table 4.5 reports the findings of one trade study in this regard. This table shows the rack jobber to be the most important source of supply for practically all of the general merchandise lines carried by the typical supermarket.

The importance of specialization in merchandising nonfoods is interesting. The supermarket is rapidly proving itself adept at selling nonfood items; however, buying skills have not been developed to any large extent. Should supermarket buyers develop

---

[97] For the operating methods and financial results of specific rack jobbers cf. "U.S. Consumer Products Rack Up New Advance in Operating Results," *Barron's*, August 23, 1965, p. 15; and "Sophistication in Supermarkets: Rack Jobbers Polish Technique," *Merchandising Week*, November 8, 1965, p. 37.

TABLE 4.5

GENERAL MERCHANDISE LINES, PER CENT OF SUPERMARKETS
HANDLING, TYPICAL NUMBER OF ITEMS, AND MAJOR
SOURCES OF SUPPLY

Merchandise Line	Per Cent of Supers Handling	Typical Number of Items	Major Source of Supply		
			Rack Jobber (Per cent)	Whole-saler (Per cent)	Manu-facturer (Per cent)
Health and Beauty Aids	99	400	46	34	20
Housewares	94	250	77	11	12
Women's Hosiery	91	15	46	28	26
Stationery	90	35	47	34	19
Magazines (general line)	88	75	56	43	1
Glassware	84	40	60	16	24
Children's Books	77	30	52	29	19
Baby Needs	76	25	54	28	18
Pet Supplies	70	50	74	15	11
Toys	69	75	78	12	10
Men's Socks	65	10	65	15	20
Children's Socks	63	10	66	15	19
Phonograph Records	55	75	85	12	3
Garden Supplies	53	25	27	44	29
Hardware	50	65	69	18	13
Underwear	50	10	71	10	19
Notions and Sundries	49	60	62	24	14
Other Soft Goods	46	50	70	11	19
Photographic Supplies	46	10	41	50	9
Greeting Cards	35	150	60	17	23
Electrical Appliances	15	20	38	44	18

Source: Super Market Institute, *The Super Market Industry Speaks*, Thirteenth Annual Report (Chicago: Super Market Institute, 1961), p. 20.

buying skills commensurate with the abilities of the rack jobber, perhaps margins could be reduced and items sold to consumers at lower prices, or margins could be left unaltered, resulting in larger profits to the supermarket firms. Perhaps, were there a stronger price competitive pressure on general merchandise lines, more supermarkets would make an effort to develop specialized buying skills for these lines.

To Make or Buy

Many supermarket operators are finding that the question of whether to purchase goods from an outsider as opposed to engaging in the manufacture of those goods is no longer outside the realm of their consideration. Some large supermarket chain organizations have long been integrated backward to sources of supply and have invested heavily in their own manufacturing facilities. Several supermarket chains have engaged extensively in manufacturing such commodities as bread, ice cream, and some dairy products.

No longer must a chain organization consist of thousands of units before manufacturing or processing of its own commodities is feasible. One small, 67-unit midwestern chain, finding that it could not get ice cream manufacturers to agree to its price and specifications, decided after careful analysis to invest in its own ice cream plant. The results, as reported by one of the chain's executives, have been rather astounding. The chain discovered that its stores could be supplied with ice cream products at a greatly reduced cost and that a better quality of ice cream could be delivered for the price.[98]

Surely, however, the degree to which a supermarket organization can economically engage in manufacturing activities is limited by many factors and conditions. Charvat lists the following factors which should be considered before determining the question of make or buy:[99]

1. Investment in manufacturing facilities required.
2. Alternative use of funds.
3. Frequency of depressed conditions in the line so that advantageous purchases can be made.
4. Total dollar volume of the specific item.
5. Total dollar volume of any one item within a line.
6. Strength of brand preference for competing products.
7. Strength of the emotional buying motive for the item as a result of strong preference.
8. Need for a yardstick to insure proper costs for the product.

The extent to which supermarket organizations are likely to engage in manufacturing activities, thus partially supplying their own merchandise needs, is uncertain. Much of this activity stems

---

[98] Personal interview with Mr. Chan Kinter, Vice President, Marsh Supermarkets, Yorktown, Indiana, Summer, 1961.
[99] Charvat, *op. cit.*

directly from the competitive nature of the business, and those products which are more frequently being manufactured by the retailer are usually highly competitive items in the store's total product mix. Therefore, if faced with more stringent competitive conditions from discount sellers or other conventional supermarkets, manufacturing activities by supermarket organizations are quite likely to increase.

Conclusions on Buying Policies and Decisions

An essential element of the supermarket's total merchandise strategy is its buying policies and skills. The chain supermarkets have developed perhaps the strongest competitive advantage in buying skills. This results undoubtedly from their ability to reap economies from highly developed specialized skills and division of labor. The most prominent of these techniques is the buying committee.

The independent supermarkets have responded by affiliating with either voluntary or cooperative chain organizations. And thus the competitive battle continues. In a highly competitive business like food retailing, if one business is able to buy merchandise even 10 cents lower on the case, this offers it a strong merchandising edge. Thus, all supermarket firms must be constantly on the alert in order to have adequate sources of supply, and be able to obtain quality merchandise with the terms and conditions of sale which will enable them to maintain a competitive condition.

Trends in Supermarket Location Policies

Location policies and decisions are another vital part of a supermarket's total merchandising strategy. Merchandising concerns itself with the planning involved in having the right merchandise available at the right time, and at the right price, and at the *right place.* The battle for desirable sites among supermarket operators is not so obvious to the uninitiated observer as is the competitive battle waged with price cuts, promotional techniques, and expanded product lines. However, this battle for sites is a natural extension of merchandising power. An aggressive real estate program is an absolute requirement for the self-preservation and survival of most supermarkets. The most astute product, promotion, and pricing policies cannot offset to any great extent a poorly located supermarket. An average new supermarket opened today may represent an investment of $450,000 or more. Surely before an investment of this size is made, unusual investigation and study will be given to the problem of where to locate the store.

. Many firms are giving increasing attention to the problem of locating new stores as well as to the process of evaluating existing store sites.

According to the Super Market Institute, the supermarkets opened in 1966 (only those stores doing $1,000,000 or more per year) represent approximately 10 per cent of all supers in operation at the end of the year.[100] *Progressive Grocer* states that 2,890 new supermarkets (stores doing in excess of $500,000 per year) were opened in 1966. These figures give some idea of the rapidly expanding supermarket field. And this expansion places greater pressures on supermarket executives to evaluate location proposals more thoroughly. Naturally, this rapid expansion means that there are fewer and fewer good sites for supermarkets, and, further, that each operator is giving increased attention to site-selection and trading-area studies before location decisions are made. The day has long since passed when site selection consisted of company executives driving around a neighborhood looking for a suitable and available vacant lot.

The Approach to Store-Location Decisions

The policy decision of where to locate supermarkets is a multiple-facet one. And, this problem confronts not only those who are considering the opening of a new store but those who are also considering relocating a store. The discussion here will center primarily on the decisions affecting new store openings.

Choosing the Community

When a large supermarket chain bent on expansion or a smaller independent who wishes to become a multi-unit operation wishes to

---

[100] *The Super Market Industry Speaks, op. cit.,* p. 4.

open additional stores, the initial problem is one of choosing a city or town in which to locate the new store.

As a partial guide in reaching a solution to the problem of the selection of a city or town in which to locate, the following points should be considered:[101]

1. Diversification of industry.
2. Permanence of industry.
3. Seasonal prosperity.
4. Community spirit.
5. Potential trading area.
6. Buying power.
7. Competition and economic need.
8. Business services and facilities.

These guides are more or less self-explanatory and represent "ideal" requirements. The supermarket executive is likely to be faced with some compromise among these guides. Stated simply, the supermarket operator desires a community which possesses average or above-average purchasing power by a large number of potential customers. These potential customers should have a reasonably high standard of living which will motivate them to buy quality goods in large amounts.

Because of the expanded scope of most supermarkets, careful attention must be given to such factors as diversification of industry and seasonal prosperity as they affect customer buying power. The relationship between customer income and food expenditures is a relatively constant one, which means that if customer incomes fall during a period of depressed business activity, company strike, or seasonal swings in an industry's business, food expenditures would fall also, but not by so large an amount as income. Today, however, many supermarkets are carrying broad assortments of luxury and other nonfood lines. A depressed period of business activity which is likely to shrink customer incomes can have tremendous effects on the supermarket's total sales, even though strictly food sales may remain relatively high.

One researcher has developed a rather unique concept to enable location analysts to evaluate given communities in terms of their

---

[101] For an excellent treatment of locational factors, see R. D. Entenberg, *Effective Retail and Market Distribution* (New York: The World Publishing Company, 1966), pp. 61-76.

potential for supermarkets. The concept deals essentially with two main factors: the amount of food sales available in any geographical area and certain characteristics of supermarket facilities in any geographical area. These two factors are then combined to form an index of supermarket saturation. This index can be defined as: an index number providing a relative measure of supermarket saturation in any given trading area. Expressed as a functional relationship:

Formula for Index of Supermarket Saturation

$$IRS_1 = \frac{C_1 \text{ x } RE_1}{RF_1}$$

Where: IRS_1 = Index of supermarket saturation for area one
C_1 = Number of consumers in area one
RE_1 = Food expenditures per consumer in area one
RF_1 = Retail facilities in area one

Consider the following example in analyzing supermarket potential in Market A:

The 100,000 consumers in Market A spend an average of $5.50 per week in food stores. There are 15 supermarkets serving Market A with a total of 144,000 square feet of selling area.

$$IRS_A = \frac{100,000 \text{ x } 5.50}{144,000} = \frac{550,000}{144,000} = \$3.82$$

The $3.82 per square foot of selling area measured against the dollars of square feet necessary to break even would provide the measure of saturation in Market A. The $3.82 figure would also be useful in evaluating relative opportunity in different market areas.

For example, if an operator was considering entering four different market areas and the IRS for each market was calculated as follows: Market area A=$3.82; Market area B=$1.76; Market area C=$2.12; and Market area D=$2.94; his course of action would be reasonably clear.

In summary, the index of supermarket saturation provides valuable insights for the supermarket operator into the evaluation of available potential in any market. It provides a superior measurement for the simple analysis of market potential, because it would take into account both the demand side (potential) and the supply side (retail facilities) in evaluating a market.[102]

Choosing the Store Site

Once the supermarket operator has settled the question of what community or town in which to locate, his next immediate problem is what sites are available and, of the available sites, which one will best fulfill the needs of his company.

A supermarket organization must appraise and evaluate the following factors before a specific site is finally chosen:

1. Type of goods in product lines.
2. Traffic arteries.
3. Traffic classification.
4. Advertising value.
5. Neighborhood appearance.
6. Retail grouping.
7. Rental values.

One supermarket operator summed up what he considered to be his company's main site location problem as follows:

> Our problem is to get between the customers and potential customers and our competition. If we can do that our site problems are whipped. However, we have two enemies fighting against the accomplishment of this task: our competition and sharp real estate operators.[103]

Certainly to be considered are the possible sites available to competitors and the saturation of these sites. From the point of view of some firms, a fair location in an area where other sites are not available might be better than a first-class site where two other excellent sites are also open to serve the same local area.

When a supermarket organization is in the process of choosing a store site, this choice may be made from the following possible types of business areas:[104]

1. *Central shopping area.* This is generally the downtown or primary shopping district. The area will include the financial and

---

[102] B. J. LaLonde, "New Frontiers in Store Location," *Supermarket Merchandising,* February, 1963, p. 110.

[103] Personal interview—respondent wished to remain anonymous.

[104] Delbert J. Duncan and Charles F. Phillips, *Retailing: Principles and Methods* (Homewood, Illinois: Richard D. Irwin, Inc., 1967), pp. 110-118.

governmental units of the community and the shopping goods institutions such as department stores.

2. *Secondary shopping area.* This type of area is similar to the central shopping area with the exception that it is smaller. Central shopping areas are generally composed of a number of secondary shopping areas.

3. *String street development.* These are minor shopping districts located along lines of radial and axial transportation routes.

4. *Neighborhood area.* This is a business area containing a cluster of convenience goods stores located within or adjacent to a small residential area.

5. *Shopping center.* This term is reserved for planned or developed centers in suburban residential neighborhoods.

Recently, many supermarket operators are being faced more and more with the alternative of choosing a solo location within either a central shopping center, secondary center, string street or neighborhood area, or going to a planned or controlled shopping center. One source estimates that there are 9,500 controlled shopping centers in the United States and that every center has at least one major supermarket.[105] Thus, controlled shopping centers have become a readily available alternative choice for supermarket firms seeking store sites.

The controlled shopping center offers many advantages to supermarkets seeking suitable store sites. In many instances, the traffic problems are largely overcome in a controlled shopping center which offers adequate parking. Downtown congestion has caused many firms to look only to controlled shopping centers as a source of suitable supermarket sites.

Controlled shopping center locations for supermarkets are considered more desirable than are solo locations because shopping centers will draw traffic from a larger radius than would any single store. One source states that controlled shopping centers will draw traffic from a trading area as far away as five to 10 miles, depending on the over-all size of the center.[106] A single store would be doing quite well if business could be drawn from a radius exceeding two miles.

Because of the glamor, attractiveness, and customer drawing

---

[105] S. O. Kaylin, 27th Annual *Chain Store Age* Survey of Construction and Modernization, *Chain Store Age* (Supermarket Executives Edition), January, 1966, p. E8.
[106] *Ibid.*

power of the controlled shopping centers, many supermarket firms have rushed to take locations in these centers just because they have been made available. There is danger, however, in this behavior. One study group concluded that shopping center locations should be given the same study and scrutiny as individual locations and above all else the center developer should not be relied on to make the trading area studies.[107]

Many of the problems affecting the downtown primary and secondary shopping areas are being overcome, and supermarket firms are looking once again to these areas for supermarket locations.[108] Traffic congestion is being alleviated by such techniques as creating malls, closing off streets, and establishing one-way traffic. Cooperative efforts stimulated by various government programs aimed at renewing and beautifying the city are also helping to revitalize downtown shopping areas, thus making them more desirable for supermarket sites.

The question of whether to locate in a controlled shopping center as opposed to a solo location is indeterminate. The issue, like other aspects of merchandising policy, depends upon the individual organization's objectives, policies, and operating philosophies. The procedure for choosing store sites will vary considerably from organization to organization,[109] but one major new consideration now appears to be permeating this decision and that is the replacement of hunch or guess methods with the use of more scientific information. The statement should not be made, however, that there is a simple scientific formula into which one merely plugs the data, punches a button, and arrives at the proper choice. Instead, the operator must constantly attempt to fill gaps in his knowledge with scientific techniques and approaches combined with imagination and ingenuity in order to make better decisions and arrive at better location choices. Some of these trends toward the more scientific use of materials and techniques merit attention here.

---

[107] "Super Market Site Selection Today's Tough Decision: SMI," *Super Market News,* November 22, 1965, p. 1.

[108] "Two Chains Try Vest Pocket Centers," *Chain Store Age,* March 1, 1967, p. 38.

[109] For a review and summary of this trend, see "The Art of Locating New Stores Seen Fast Becoming a Science: SMI Annual Convention," *Super Market News,* May 17, 1965, p. 33.

Trends in Supermarket Location Techniques and Decisions

A recent issue of a well-known supermarket publication carried a feature story on the use of economic and marketing geography as a tool to aid in store-site selection problems.[110] This concept of economic and marketing geography is now being hailed as a highly effective technique.

Originally, supermarket operators relied on intuition in the selection of sites. However, with mushrooming populations and increased number of stores, such intuition was sometimes erroneous and instilled a false sense of security.

As time progressed, intuition was frequently replaced with experience, but this too is often a poor guide because of lack of comparables, and limited size of many organizations. However, large chains such as Kroger still rely heavily on past experience and utilize a technique for helping make site decisions which is called the "concept of similarity of experience." Simply put, the concept means that out of 1,400 stores one can find a good many similar, if not identical, situations. Consequently, when Kroger is evaluating a store site, this site is related to as many comparable operations of the chain as is possible.[111]

Most supermarket executives today realize that the best approach to site selection is research and more research. The scientific investigation of suitable store sites is more and more coming to be called "marketing geography."[112]

Marketing geography is concerned with two important dimensions of the problem of site selection:[113]

1. The boundaries of the over-all trading area.
2. An understanding of how the trading area is subdivided into components.

To gain an understanding of these two important aspects of the problem and thus make better decisions regarding the choice of store sites, many of the larger supermarket firms have developed

---

[110] "A New Dimension: Economic and Marketing Geography," *Food Topics,* March, 1961, p. 6.

[111] "Some Real Estate Considerations," *Super Market Merchandising,* August, 1959, p. 71.

[112] "A New Dimension: Economic and Marketing Geography," *op. cit.,* p. 8.

[113] For an expanded and detailed treatment of the concept of marketing geography, see William Applebaum and Saul B. Cohen, "Store Trading Areas in a Changing Market," *Journal of Retailing,* Fall, 1961, p. 14.

real estate divisions which employ urban economists, real estate experts, and geographers. These people are utilizing the techniques of the various sciences and disciplines to enable them to make more defensible decisions. Many firms which cannot afford the expense of a full-time real estate division are utilizing on a consulting basis people and firms possessing these skills.

Among the special skills and techniques of these marketing geographers are the following which are being utilized extensively:

1. *Mathematical models.* These are usually complex models consisting of parameters and objectives. Such devices as linear programming, transportation models, and others are based on known or discoverable logistics. Optimum decisions are the general result.

2. *Economic base analysis.* Economic base analysis provides a method for estimating future population trends and the potential demands for various types of land uses in any city. The steps may be summarized thus:[114]

    a. Ascertain the number of urban growth or basic employees in each industry or trade.

    b. Subtract the number of urban growth or basic employees in each industry or trade from the total employed workers in order to determine the number of service employees.

    c. Calculate the ratio between basic and service employment.

    d. Calculate the percentage of total employment to the total population of the metropolitan area being studied as of the last available census. This percentage usually ranges from 41 to 47 per cent.

    e. By interviewing the managers of principal basic industries, or by taking into account past trends, make an estimate of the probable future total number of basic employees.

    f. Estimate future population of the entire metropolitan area by applying the percentage of employment to population that prevailed in a given year or on the basis of some other selected percentage if this seems warranted.

    g. Estimate future total employment of the metropolitan area by applying the ratio of basic employment to total employment now existing or by adjusting this ratio for changed conditions.

    h. To estimate the amount of land required for new commercial centers, calculate the square feet of floor area required in department stores, variety stores, supermarkets, apparel stores, and all other types of stores to handle the volume of sales created by the added population, and also allow a 4 to 1 ratio between parking and selling area.

---

[114] Arthur M. Weimer and Homer Hoyt, *Principles of Real Estate,* Third Edition (New York: The Ronald Press Co., 1954), p. 357.

3. *Aerial photography.* This is simply taking pictures from air-
planes and blowing them up to large size for inspection of
traffic arteries and the extent of property development. The
main advantage of aerial photography is that it enables the
viewer to stand back, so to speak, and view a large geographical
area with one glance, thus getting a better perspective.[115]

Of course, there are other devices which may be employed by
scientific researchers to aid management in making better store-
site decisions. And a logical assumption is that better techniques
are yet to be developed. The important point to consider is that
store-site selection, like the other variables of a firm's merchandising
strategy, can be decided intuitively and arbitrarily. But in light of
today's competitive environment, firms which make decisions on
this basis may not be long in the market place.

One researcher, whose work has been previously cited and who
has contributed most significantly to location theory concepts, concludes that firms employing location research in their expansion
planning expect basically two things from the research:[116]

1. An evaluation of specific sites as to their sales potential and the
   probability of a store's long-range success at the site.
2. A store-location strategy plan or model that undertakes to select,
   from among the location alternatives in a given geographic area,
   those locations that will produce for the firm an optimum share of
   market potential, a minimum hazard for future sales erosion, and a
   maximum return on total investment over the lease period.

Applebaum further states that where a firm seeks to improve
or expand its market, proposes to open stores in a new territory,
or considers an acquisition, there are several fundamental factors
or criteria to be analyzed and evaluated.[117]

1. Define the Objective. A store-location strategy study cannot
   be undertaken without a knowledge of a firm's business policies.
2. Analyze the Economic Base. It is essential to obtain relevant
   information about the economic base of the area—economic activities, employment characteristics, past trends and future prospects.
3. Study the Population and Its Characteristics. Alexander Pope
   once commented that "the proper study of mankind is man." The
   proper study of most marketing phenomena also centers around
   "man."

---

[115] "The Uses of Aerial Photography," *Super Market Merchandising,* May, 1960,
p. 63.
[116] William Applebaum, "Guidelines for a Store-Location Strategy Study," *Journal of Marketing,* Vol. 30, October, 1966, p. 42.
[117] *Ibid.,* pp. 42-45.

4. Ascertain the Environmental Conditions. This consideration includes such factors as terrain features, road network, land uses, retail business centers, etc.

5. Make an Inventory of Competition. Because competition exists everywhere and because it is dynamic, competition requires a field survey.

6. Appraise Competition. Study both the strength and weakness of competition including finances and management.

7. Study Consumer Attitude. Such a study should attempt to discover the consumer "image" of your own firm.

8. Study Your Own Company's Market Coverage and Penetration. If necessary utilize customer interviews and "store spottings."

9. Analyze Your Own Store's Performance. This means essentially a detailed analysis of store operating expenses and, perhaps, a management audit.

10. Appraise Your Own Store Facilities and Locations. This involves appraising the adequacy of each of the company's store facilities as well as possible locations for the short and long run.

11. Study Areas of Underpenetration. Study areas not presently served or served inadequately.

12. Consider Competitors' Likely Location Moves. Try to step into the other fellow's shoes and try to guess what he might do.

13. Develop a Store-Location Strategy Plan. This amounts to a comprehensive plan of action.

14. Calculate Your Own Company's Future Position in the Area. Assuming your strategy works out, what will be the likely consequences to your company?

15. Project Investment Requirements, Profits, and Return on Investment. This amounts to both a forecast and a review of previous decisions.

16. Prepare a Written Report. This is done, mainly, to allow the researcher to subject his analysis to some objective and judicious criticism.

Such a comprehensive series of checkpoints or guidelines would surely eliminate much of the risk and uncertainty from store-location decisions. However, even such a comprehensive and exhaustive approach is no guarantee that optimum decisions will be made. For any given situation, the individual decision maker will have to exercise his judgment as to how much to cover under each suggested step or, in total, what techniques to use to supplement his individual judgment and experience in making decisions regarding locational strategy.

Summary

The primary responsibility of supermarket managements is to develop and implement sound merchandising strategies. That is, the supermarket manager must develop comprehensive plans which will enable the store to compete and operate effectively within its competitive environment. Merchandising is the technique or planning involved in having the right goods at the right place, at the right time, and at the right price. Supermarket executives must be first and foremost merchandisers. And not only must the executives be imbued with a merchandising philosophy, but subordinates as well must be made aware of their merchandising responsibilities. The economic justification of the supermarket is that by virtue of the marketing functions performed, the institution adds value to the merchandise.

The supermarket's success or failure is to a large degree determined by the products merchandised. However, not only must the supermarket buyer determine what products to carry, he must also concern himself with decisions pertaining to optimum space allocation and utilization, make brand decisions and policies, and cope with the increasingly complex problem of how to merchandise general food lines.

The severe competitive nature of supermarket merchandising calls for increasing attention to price policies and decisions by the supermarket operator. Variable markup strategies are rapidly coming to dominate this area of merchandising decisions. The task of getting the large number of shoppers into the market—an absolute necessity for all supermarkets—is largely the job of promotion. Many astute managers are giving increasing attention to their in-store promotional policies and decisions. This awareness results, perhaps, from the large number of industry studies which have shown the effective results of well-planned, in-store promotions and displays.

The supermarket operator must be constantly alert to practice sound buying procedures and techniques. In an industry characterized by penny profits, a buying economy which results in a very slight saving can be something of a boon to the year's operation.

Finally, supermarket organizations are giving increasing attention to the selection of suitable store sites. The day of intuitive decision making in this area has passed. High development costs, increased competition, decline in favorable sites, and better experiences with past location decisions are causing many organizations to look for more scientific approaches and solutions to this problem.

Chapter 5

The Supermarket in the Seventies

SUPERMARKETS HAVE come a long way from their humble pine board, abandoned factory beginnings to a situation where, today, they have expensive fixtures and opulent architectural trappings. The supermarket is the number-one food merchandiser in the United States and presently accounts for over 70 per cent of total grocery store sales. The next important question becomes: "Where does the supermarket go from here?" What of the future? What are some factors that may limit growth? These are a few of the issues to be explored in this chapter.

Food Retailing in the Seventies

One does not have to look far to discover prognostications about the food retailing industry in the decade of the seventies. With a comprehensive trade literature, active trade associations, and articulate industry leaders, activity in the food field has been frequently forecast. As we move into the waning phase of the 1960's, curiosity is growing over what lies ahead. As we have seen, during the past decade the nation's marketplace has been transformed in many important ways. We have witnessed an explosive growth of the youth market, an upgrading of educational achievements, a pronounced shift to white collar employment, and, perhaps most significant, an imposing reshuffling of income distribution.

Without question, these important changes and their continued development will have an important bearing on food sales and distribution. In order that we might better understand the future of food distribution, let us review briefly some rather important factors which will affect it.[1]

By 1975, there will be close to 225 million Americans. And while population is some index of economic activity, it must be remembered that the markets of the seventies are people *plus* purchasing power. The mix of population, however, given the necessary income will, in turn, greatly affect food distribution from products to methods.

More persons will reach age 20 in 1967 than any other time in the nation's history. From here on in, and for the next 10 years, the population of young adults will increase a great deal faster than the total population.

Between 1965 and 1975, persons between 18 and 24 will increase in number by over 35 per cent, or more than twice as fast as our total population. Meanwhile, persons between 35 and 54 will actually decline in number, while the population of those 55 and over will increase by about the average rate.

During the first part of the seventies, the family population will rise by an estimated 1.0 million a year. In 1975, there will be roughly 57 million families in the U.S., compared with roughly 48 million in 1967. About two thirds of this growth will be accounted for by young families—that is, where the head is under 35. This segment of the family population will increase by some 50 per cent between 1965 and 1975.

Because of the nation's changing social values, the postwar generation has acquired appreciably more schooling than the previous one. The number of persons completing high school as well as the number going on to college has risen rather astoundingly. Today about 19 million adults have had at least some exposure to college; by 1975 it is estimated that they will number 27 million, or about 40 per cent more.

One of the most significant developments which has affected,

---

[1] The material of this section is based largely upon the projections found in Chapter 3. Highlights from two other sources are also incorporated into this section. See Fabian Linden, "The Nation's Marketplace in 1975. . . Growing Younger and Richer," *The Conference Board Record,* Vol. IV, No. 5, May, 1967, pp. 44-47, and Phillip M. Hauser, "Is the Market Moving Away from You?" *A View to 1970,* Super Market Institute Proceedings of the 1965 Mid-Year Conference, pp. 10-13.

and will continue to affect, our economy is the reshuffling or changing distribution of incomes.

Households with incomes of $3,000 a year are fewer than 10 years ago. The income pyramid is in the process of being inverted. About a decade ago, approximately 70 per cent of all families earned $7,000 or less, but by 1965, the ratio had declined to about 50 per cent, and by 1975, it is expected to decrease to about 36 per cent. Ten years ago, families with more than $10,000 a year accounted for 30 per cent of total demand, but by 1975, the proportion is estimated to exceed two thirds.

Many families have attained upper-income class status by virtue of the wives' earnings. In half of all homes with incomes of $10,000 to $15,000 a year, the woman of the house goes to work. By 1975, it is estimated that close to two out of every five married women will be earning a pay check.

The implications of these vast and sweeping impending demographic and economic changes are far reaching and of such magnitude and importance as to warrant discussion throughout the chapter. However, briefly stated, the more immediate and direct implications are these. The market in terms of number of customers and potential customers is large. The mass market has become a series of mass markets; there are innumerable market segments to which the individual food store might direct its promotions and appeals. The mass markets are rapidly becoming class markets. An ever larger proportion of personal income is available for discretionary spending, for comforts and luxuries. The American consumer is the best fed in the world. His tastes and desires for food and grocery products are ever-expanding.

As the family income rises, each additional dollar of earnings is spent differently than the last. As incomes increase and essential needs are satisfied, extra earnings become available for the goods and services that make for a more pleasant life. Consequently, with the expected increment in average family spending, and with more families being catapulted into the middle- and upper-earnings brackets, one can anticipate some appreciable changes in the composition of the family's market basket.

In the recent past, for each 1 per cent increment in real disposable income, outlays for food moved up by less than half a percentage point. This would imply that food store operators, unless they are quick to add nonfood lines and expand the range of their customer services, may enjoy something less than the full prosperity which the above generalizations tend to portray.

No tomorrow is exactly like yesterday, but the past does tell us something about the future. What, then, is the future of grocery store sales and, of course, the supermarket, which is the primary outlet for these sales? One area which appears to capture the imagination of many forecasters is: "What are food and grocery sales likely to be in 1975?" Sales forecasts are likely to differ markedly from individual to individual, depending, of course, on the techniques employed and the various assumptions underlying the forecasts. However, should grocery store sales continue to increase in the future as they have in the past at the rate of about 5 to 6 per cent a year, grocery store sales will quite likely be around $88 billion in 1970 and $110 billion in 1975.[2]

One creditable industry source is not quite as optimistic in forecasting total grocery store sales to 1975, inasmuch as it concludes that sales for this period are likely to reach only $100.1 billion.[3] Table 5.1 is a condensation of the *Progressive Grocer* projections of several dimensions of food retailing to 1975.

As can be seen both from Table 5.1 and from the previous discussion, the outlook for the food and grocery business in the coming decade appears cheerful for a number of reasons. Several factors seem to militate for a prosperous and dynamic decade for grocery retailing. Rather unusual, if not remarkable, increases in consumers' per capita and per family income plus the rapid growth in the number of consuming units, *i.e.*, individuals and households, should bolster retail grocery sales significantly. Only an internal economic recession of some consequence or an international disaster could appreciably dampen the outlook for grocery sales during the 1970's.

---

[2] These are the author's own estimates based upon an average growth rate of about 5.7 per cent per year and extrapolated to the respective years.
[3] "Food Retailing 1975—A Look into the Future," *Progressive Grocer*, April, 1966, pp. 165-170.

TABLE 5.1

Food Industry Projections to 1975

	1965	1975	Per Cent Increase
Grocery store sales (in billions)	65.8	100.1	52
Supermarkets	46.5	75.1	62
Superettes	8.6	15.2	77
Small stores	10.7	9.8	−8
Number of grocery stores	227,050	216,000	−5
Supermarkets	31,750	42,000	32
Superettes	28,300	32,000	13
Small stores	167,000	142,000	−15
Average sales per supermarket	1,465,000	2,400,000	64
Per cent of disposable income	19	19	------
Average supermarket total area (square feet)	10,800	13,300	23
Average selling area	7,500	10,800	44
New stores built	5,135	55,000 (through 1975)	
New supermarkets	2,710	30,000 (through 1975)	

Source: Adapted from "Food Retailing 1975: A Look into the Future," *Progressive Grocer,* April, 1966, p. 169.

Supermarkets Look to the Seventies

In light of the dynamic and optimistic forecasts for grocery retailing in the seventies, what about the role of the supermarket in selling these food and grocery products? The truth is there are many signs which point to a not-so-glamorous decade of the 1970's for supermarkets.

M. P. McNair has described a kind of cycle in the life and functioning of retail institutions in the following terms:

An innovator has a new kind of distinctive enterprise. . . . He attracts the public on the basis of the price appeal made possible by the low operating costs inherent in his innovation. . . . He trades up, improves the quality of his merchandise, improves the appearance and standing of his store, attains greater respectability. Then comes the period of growth. . . . The maturity phase soon tends to be followed by top heaviness, too great conservatism, a decline in the rate of return on investment and eventual vulnerability. Vulnerability to what? Vulnerability to the next revolution of the wheel, to the next fellow who has a bright idea and who starts his business on a low cost basis, slipping in under the umbrella the old line institutions have hoisted.[4]

Longer-run observations of retail merchandising and the emergence and development of retailing institutions seem to reveal a rhythm or cycle of evolution. This rhythm or cycle appears as alternating movement in the dominant method of operations. On the one hand can be witnessed the tendency toward specialization of function performed, or of the merchandise handled by individual firms. On the other hand, the movement is away from such specialization toward the integration of related activities under a single management or the diversification of products handled by a single firm. Hollander refers to this phenomenon as the "retail accordion."[5] His descriptive label, of course, implies the alternating contraction and expansion in the cycle or evolution of retail trade. Whether it be called the "wheel of retailing" or the "retail accordion," the message is ultimately the same: there is nothing static about retail merchandising, no institution is immune to growth and change, growth and change are products of innovation, and consumers are exceedingly receptive to innovation and, thus, change. As a matter of fact, food store distribution as a system and food stores as the institutions offer near-perfect examples of both the concepts of the "wheel of retailing" and the "retail accordion." No later than 50 years ago, one could witness extreme specialization in both systems and institutions. The emergence of the food supermarket with emphasis not only on food but a wider range of consumer products was an example of a movement away from specialization, as well as an example of the turned wheel toward a more efficient and lower cost method of distribution, *i.e.,* innovation.

The more recent period has seen a tendency toward wider and more scrambled assortments. The supermarkets have invaded the nonfood field, the discount merchandisers have added soft lines, and the variety chains have broadened assortments and traded up their merchandise classifications. The logic of these developments, in most instances, has been economic. Scrambling of merchandise lines

---

[4] A. B. Smith (ed.), "Significant Trends and Developments in the Postwar Period," *Competitive Distribution in a Free High-Level Economy and its Implications for the University* (Pittsburgh: University of Pittsburgh Press, 1958), pp. 17-18.

[5] Stanley C. Hollander, "Notes on the Retail Accordion," *Journal of Retailing,* Summer, 1966, pp. 29-40.

has been appealing to both seller and buyer. The seller, of course, is enticed to scramble because of the incentive for marginal or incremental profits; the buyer or customer is attracted by what Baranoff calls "concentrated variety" or the assembly of everything under one roof.[6] Such concentration for the consumer means, at least up to a given point, increased shopping or buying efficiency, as a result of reduced shopping inputs such as time, money, and energy.

History and development, however, can never be long arrested in their march toward the future. It is unlikely that the ideal or optimum method of food distribution has been attained. Neither is it likely or logical to assume that history consists of a few constantly recurring patterns. What we see most often in a new development is a slight and fleeting resemblance of what has gone before, whereas close surveillance reveals new trends, new forces, brought about by new and different environmental conditions. Thus "the wheel" does not revolve a constant set of recurring patterns. The exact methods of food distribution employed during the 1920's and 1930's are not likely to reappear. Instead, given a dynamic system, we are most likely to encounter new methods, new systems, and new institutions in the future. The supermarket can easily be recognized as a retail institution that has evolved much the same as McNair describes in his "wheel of retailing" example. Is food marketing now, however, about to witness the next turning of the wheel? Has the supermarket hoisted an umbrella under which the next new competitor might slip? There are several trends and conditions prevalent in supermarket operations today which may imply that the supermarket is becoming more vulnerable to new ideas and new forms of competition.

The Changing Role of the Supermarket

During the 1960's, supermarkets added many new nonfood lines and expanded nonfood sales as a percentage of total sales. In doing this, they sold the nonfoods at the full list prices of the conventional retailers whose lines they added. Women's hosiery, for example, was sold at the same prices at which it was merchan-

---
[6] Seymour Baranoff, "Retailing As an Operating System," in Reavis Cox, Wroe Alderson, and Stanley Shapiro, eds., *Theory in Marketing,* 2nd Series (Homewood, Illinois: Richard D. Irwin, Inc., 1964), p. 161.

dised in department stores. Supermarket customers, while shopping food lines, were given the opportunity to buy nonfoods on a convenience basis. These customers could consequently purchase numerous soft goods lines and other general merchandise lines without making special trips to the conventional retailers of these lines. As the number of nonfood lines in supermarkets increased, the supermarket became, foremost, a convenience store, and much of its appeal was changed to a convenience basis. The result, of course, has increased the vulnerability of the supermarket to another institution featuring lower prices or basing its appeal on more of a price basis. Also, many of the newer nonfood lines introduced into the supermarket's product mix were slower turnover items, requiring special handling, or facilities which tended to increase expenses. Other factors, as well, increased the operating expense ratio of supermarkets.

During the 1960's, the supermarket added spacious parking lots, air conditioning, and expensive fixtures. The uses of give-aways, such as trading stamps and other premiums, were expanded as promotional devices. And delicatessen types of food, much broader assortments of a number of product lines, including cheese, wines, and other gourmet products, were introduced. The result was that the supermarket, although it may have been able to absorb the added costs of one or two of these changes, could not absorb them all without increasing operating-expense ratios. Consequently, these ratios have risen from 11 to around 20 per cent. To offset this increase, gross margins, by necessity, have been increased from around 12 to 22 per cent. The implication of this increase is that supermarkets have been made even more susceptible to new forms of competition.

From 1950 to 1965, supermarkets increased their share of the grocery business from about 40 to 70 per cent. During this period, the supermarkets consistently gained market shares at the expense of the higher cost "mom and pop" clerk-service grocery stores. But with the exception of the newer version of this operation, the ultramodern drive-in and bantam markets, competition from these smaller grocery stores has rapidly dwindled.

From 1960 to 1965, the potential average number of people served by each new supermarket has dropped from 7,300 to 3,600, or less than half of the former total. Each supermarket opened last year found itself in direct competition with at least three other super-markets, and the new supermarkets added in 1965 represented 9 per cent of all supermarkets in operation at the end of the year.[7]

Thus the rapid growth and expansion in the recent past of supermarkets has in many respects limited their opportunities for growth and expansion in the future. There are other signs or trends which suggest that not all bodes well for the supermarket.

Other Supermarket Problems

Many chains have cut back considerably from their peak rate of new store building, and the stores presently being built are smaller. The growth in size of the supermarket appears to have ended, at least for several years to come. During the 1970's, oper-ators will build less hastily, will design and size the supermarket to the trading area more carefully.

Some security analysts have been demoting the supermarket stocks from the growth category. One financial authority, in appraising the supermarket industry, spoke as follows:

> There appear to be some trends in narrowing of operating margins and lagging year to year sales which can be attributed only to the inherent problems of the industry—notably overexpansion in certain areas and inability to control rising operating costs.[8]

These rising operating costs have narrowed profit margins excessively in spite of the fact that many store units do over 50 per cent of their total volume in high-margin nonfoods. On a strict merchandising basis the net-profit percentage performance has been down for a decade; in the few instances where the net-profit percentage has picked up, this has happened more because of what might be called "corporation aspects" (mergers, real estate, etc.) than because of efficient merchandising.

Supermarket margins have gradually increased from about 17 per cent in 1950 to a current 21 or 22 per cent, and some industry

---

[7] Super Market Institute, *The Super Market Industry Speaks,* Eighteenth Annual Report (Chicago: Super Market Institute, 1966), p. 15.
[8] "Wall Street Says," *Super Market Merchandising,* August, 1965, p. 30.

sources look for them to go as high as 23 to 25 per cent by 1975.[9]

In 1928, during the reign of the small clerk-service economy stores, margins averaged only about 26 per cent of sales. Could these present high and rising margins imply that the supermarket may be becoming more and more vulnerable to a new, lower cost method of food distribution?

And, finally, the strongest of the many proponents of supermarket food shopping—the housewife—is beginning to appear somewhat disenchanted with supermarket operation. In a nationwide survey of 12,394 housewives, asked "Do you like to shop in supermarkets?" the women responded as follows: "No," 51 per cent; "Yes," 40 per cent; "No opinion," 9 per cent. When a nearly identical study was made during 1952, 54 per cent of the respondents answered that they liked to shop in supermarkets. This figure declined to 48 per cent in a similar study during 1957.[10]

All those who expressed misgivings about shopping in supermarkets were asked: "Why don't you like to shop in supermarkets?" Following are the most prevailing reasons:

1. Too crowded.
2. Check-out takes too long.
3. Employees are not cheerful, helpful.
4. Product labels are not informative.
5. Prices are too high for self-service.
6. Frozen foods not frozen.
7. Fatiguing to go around the store—floors too hard.
8. Too many products; leads to confusion.
9. Takes too long to shop.
10. Manager not accessible.

A word of caution about this particular study. Asking the question, "Do you like shopping in supermarkets?" is a bit like asking a man, "Do you like to mow Scott's grass?" For a large number of housewives, shopping anywhere is a chore, not a pleasure.

Further, even though this study purports to be representative of housewives' attitudes, one should be cautious about foredooming the supermarket. Perhaps, these grievances are slight and can be overcome by better supermarket merchandising policies. In this

[9] For a comprehensive discussion of food store profits, see "Profits of Food Retailers," Chapter 15 in *Organization and Competition in Food Retailing*, Technical Study No. 7, National Commission on Food Marketing, June, 1966, pp. 277-305.

[10] *Women Speak Their Minds on Supermarkets*, a nationwide survey conducted by the Research Department of Paramount Paper Products, Omaha, Nebraska, 1961.

same study, when the respondents were asked, "Where do you shop for food?" 86 per cent said, "in a supermarket." Perhaps this reply is more indicative of the housewives' true attitude about supermarkets.

However, there is one important index which is somewhat indicative of the housewife's dissatisfaction with her supermarket, and this is her degree of store loyalty. A recent series of studies by Burgoyne Index, Inc., shows that Mrs. Consumer continues to skip around from one store to another, with 71 per cent of Burgoyne's sample shopping in more than one store to satisfy their demands for specials, variety, and quality. The majority of consumers, 56 per cent, shop in two stores; 29 per cent in three; 12 per cent in four; and 3 per cent in five or more. This, at least, would indicate that while the consumer is responsive to appeals from other stores and is willing to experiment with other store offerings, she might just as well be equally responsive and experimentally inclined toward new and different methods and institutions for food and grocery merchandising.[11]

The Food-Discount Merchandisers

One of the persistent criticisms of both independent and chain supermarkets is the degree of sameness that exists among the institutions. This sameness is said to exist not only in the physical or architectural sense, but also to a great degree in terms of merchandise strategies, such as prices, promotion, and product policies. All are pretty much the same in the average supermarket. One story which dramatizes this sameness of operation is that told of the president of a great food chain who upbraided a store manager—and was chagrined to discover that it was not one of his stores.

There are, however, several new forms of supermarket operation which differ markedly from their more conventional competitors. These are the new food-discount merchandisers and they operate in varying ways. Sometimes these stores exist as single separate entities, simply as food supermarkets selling at discount prices. In other instances, the stores exist as part of a more comprehensive arrange-

---

[11] "Consumer Attitude Survey," *Food Topics*, January, 1965, pp. 42-43.

ment of store groups, or leased departments, in what are frequently called discount department stores or omnibus stores. These two arrangements may be either open- or closed-membership stores. Open membership, of course, means that the store caters and appeals to a general buying public.

The closed-membership store, in an attempt to develop an aura of exclusiveness or belonging to a select group, sells memberships on a fee basis running from $2.00 per year to $2.00 for a lifetime membership. To qualify for membership, one must generally belong to a branch of the armed services on either an active or reserve basis, or be a federal or state employee such as post-office worker, school teacher, or civil service employee.

In most instances, the membership or closed-door operation is part of a discount department store arrangement.[12] The open-membership stores are often just individual supermarket food stores with especial low-price appeals.[13]

The discount department store with a large supermarket operation is somewhat difficult to describe. The nature and characteristics of these stores differ significantly from operation to operation and from region to region. A cross section of these new merchandising innovations is as follows:

Indianapolis, Indiana

L. S. Ayres & Co. has opened a new 150,000-square-foot department store to feature lower prices than those found in the typical department store. These new operations are called Ayre-Way Stores, and they feature a 30,000-square-foot supermarket operation at special discount prices. The Ayre-Way centers' supermarket operation is run by Scot Lad Foods, Inc., a large Chicago food wholesaler.

Denver, Colorado

The Denver area boasts several discount department store operations featuring full-scale supermarkets and selling on a closed-door or membership basis. A brief run down of two of these operations is as follows:

GEM. Government Employee's Mart is a 100,000-square-foot store with a 15,000-square-foot supermarket. The operation is open from 12:00 to 9:00 p.m. on weekdays and on Saturdays from 9:00

---

[12] During the latter part of the 1960's, the closed-membership store has gradually changed its operation to an open-membership basis.

[13] Much of the information presented here pertaining to discount food merchandisers is a result of the author's first-hand research and investigation in a number of areas including Indianapolis, Indiana; Denver, Colorado; and Los Angeles, California. Other information was gathered through trade studies and publications.

a.m. to 6:00 p.m. There are no Sunday openings. The supermarket here is owned by Red Owl, a large Minneapolis-based food chain.

GO-LO. The GO-LO store is an 80,000-square-foot department store center with an 8,400-square-foot supermarket. This operation is somewhat unique in that the supermarket is not a leased department. Merchandise resources for the supermarket are obtained from Associated Grocers of California.

Los Angeles, California

Discount department store-supermarket operations began and have thrived in the Los Angeles market area. Typical of the stores in this area is the Big A Discount Department Store. This operation contains 112,000 square feet of selling space with 52 departments and does around $22,000,000 annual volume. Several of the departments are leased to independents as is the case with the 34,000-square-foot discount supermarket which is run by Food Company, Inc. Every item that is not controlled by the state of California is retailed 10 to 11 per cent lower than the average super.

One might ask: "Why the concern with discount department store-supermarket operations?" The answer, upon examining closely the methods and appeals of these operations, becomes obvious. These new methods and others are likely to alter conventional supermarket merchandising strategies and techniques significantly. They pose a rather serious threat to the continued success and existence of the conventional supermarket.

Traffic is the prime requirement in the discount merchandise operation, and the food discounter has learned that food and traffic are synonymous. Furthermore, the discount house has learned that if the supers can sell nonfoods to food traffic, then certainly the discount house should be able to sell food to nonfood traffic.

Food at discount prices has an unusual appeal to the average housewife for a number of reasons; food expenditures usually average as much as one quarter to one fifth of the average household's total expenditures.[14] Therefore, if a customer feels she can save 10 to 15 per cent on her weekly food bill, she sees this as a dollar savings of $120 to $150 per year. And the frequency of food purchases is high. Thus when the customer shops for food and can make a saving from buying at a discount supermarket, this appeal is frequently reinforced.

Discount supermarkets have adopted a number of merchandising

---

[14] *Life Study of Consumer Expenditures* (New York: Time, Inc., 1957), p. 15.

techniques to enable them to sell food at discount prices. Multiple pricing, such as pricing four 10¢ bars of soap at four for 39¢, is practiced to a wide extent in an effort to do what the conventional supermarkets have been attempting to do for years—increase the size of the average customer order. By stressing every-day low prices, traffic is spread out over the entire week, and this makes for greater efficiency and utilization of resources. Customers do not have to wait for week-end specials.

Many small-sized items are entirely omitted from stock in an attempt to streamline variety. The number of shelf facings is also reduced, and those items stocked are generally the best-moving items and also well-advertised brands. In meat, no special cuts or services are provided, and only one grade is stocked. Discount supermarkets have shied away from the extensive use of trading stamps and claim a savings of as much as 2 per cent from this policy.[15]

Finally, in an effort to get the full drawing power of discount food prices, supermarket departments in some cases are leased to a food operator who does not pay any rent, but is actually subsidized by 2 or 3 per cent of sales.

In sum, comparisons of operating statements by supermarket owners now experimenting with food concessions in discount centers show the largest reduction in expense items as follows: (1) the discontinuance of the use of trading stamps, (2) reduced labor expense, and (3) use of less advertising.[16]

Shopping at a discount department store supermarket center can be a family affair. Father can shop for hardware, get his hair cut, or service his car while the children ride the amusement vehicles, and mother, after getting a permanent wave and buying the back-to-school clothes, can pick up the weekly grocery supplies.

The appeal of the shopping convenience as well as the low price is a strong one for the average consumer. Most supermarkets can only hope to draw traffic from as far away as one or two miles. However, the supermarket that is a part of a large discount department store operation may draw traffic from as far away as 30 to 40 miles.

[15] Robert J. Menichiello, "The Real Challenge of Food Discounters," *Journal of Marketing,* Vol. 31, April, 1967, pp. 37-42.
[16] *Ibid.,* p. 39.

From a virtual zero share of the market in the late 1950's, the discount supermarket is likely to control as much as 20 to 25 per cent of retail grocery store sales by 1975, given the continuation of present growth. A recent survey among members of the Super Market Institute revealed that 15 per cent of the companies operate what they consider a discount supermarket. All of the discount supers combined made up 9 per cent of the SMI member supermarkets in 1965. This compares with 5 per cent only one year earlier. The same survey revealed that 11 per cent of the members planned to open discount centers in the future.[17]

The discount center is making rather serious inroads into the field of supermarkets. Just as the supermarket replaced the small chain stores, the discount center *may* replace the supermarket as we know it today, and the takeover may come about as conventional supers move more extensively into nonfoods and department stores and others move to food distribution.[18]

Discount food supermarkets will continue to affect the conventional supermarket in essentially two respects. First, the discount operation is likely to undermine the conventional merchandising base of supermarkets and lead to much more aggressive price competition. A number of studies have been undertaken to determine if discounters can actually undersell conventional supermarkets. Most studies conclude that the discounter does effectively shade supermarket food prices.[19] Many supermarkets, unwilling to adapt to this new form of competition, are likely to succumb. Second, the trend to discount department store supermarket centers and the practice of leasing these supermarket operations may penalize those operators who are unable to get locations. This is in many ways no different than any other locational risk or advantage that may or may not accrue to the store. However, a rather frequent practice of many discount center developers is not to lease to chain supermarket operators. This situation may be overcome as chains decide to open and develop their own discount centers.

---

[17] *The Super Market Industry Speaks, op. cit.,* p. 19.

[18] "Neilson Surveys Food Discounting," *Super Market Merchandising,* January, 1965, p. 5.

[19] "The Real Challenge of Food Discounters," *op. cit.,* p. 37.

Supermarkets Face Other Forms of Competition

In addition to the discount supermarkets which are rapidly developing and expanding, and the discount department store supermarkets, or what are sometimes called super general stores or omnibus stores, the supermarket is faced with other forms of competition, all eager to increase their share of the food business.

Convenience Stores

These small-scale operators—especially the drive-in food superettes—are likely to continue to expand and to pose an ever-constant threat to the larger supermarkets.

Interest is likely to continue in these small operations for a number of reasons. First, desirable sites for full-sized supermarkets are less plentiful, and in areas which are already crowded with larger-scale stores, the superette offers a possible solution to the expansion problem. For many shoppers, these new, smartly styled, scientifically designed, easy-to-shop operations have a strong appeal, even though they have limited lines. In 1966, nearly 28,500 of these small-scale operations were in existence. Though not a serious threat to supermarkets, one must remember that these units probably get some customer dollars that otherwise would be spent in supermarkets.[20]

The Case-Lot Wholesaler

Some additional competition comes from the case-lot wholesaler, who, essentially, permits customers to shop his warehouse and make merchandise selections from stocks. Only full cases, or in some instances, half cases, are sold. Customers pay cash and carry away their own merchandise.

The incentive for the customer is lower prices through his multiple-item purchases, and the wholesaler justifies the practice on the basis of added revenues which result from these retail sales. However, regular customers of these wholesalers (the retail stores) are generally quite unhappy with these policies, and loss of retail store patronage may be the result.

---

[20] "Small Size . . . . Big Success," *Food Topics,* April, 1965, p. 18.

Another variation to the case-lot "wholesaler" is the retail store that attempts to sell quantities of distress merchandise in a bargain basement or annex. Here again, merchandising emphasis is on lower prices which supposedly result from two conditions: (1) distress or unbranded merchandise, and (2) case or half-case quantity sales. Most operators sell on a cash-and-carry basis; however, some California firms are experimenting with telephone orders and bank-credit financing.

Government Commissaries

Even government commissaries are viewed as threatening somewhat the full potential of the food supermarket. In effect, a commissary is nothing other than a supermarket operated by a branch of the armed forces. The main difference, however, between commissary stores and the conventional private enterprise supermarket is that the commissary is heavily subsidized with tax dollars. Commissary prices are established by merchandise cost plus a surcharge, usually 3 per cent. The surcharge pays only for equipment and supplies. Land, labor, building, and utilities are supplied by the installation and are paid for with tax dollars.

In 1961, there were some 259 commissaries operating within the United States, doing a volume of around $400,000,000.[21] Because commissary prices are so close to cost, this figure understates the importance of commissary sales.

Thus, the supermarket does not stand alone as the sole competitor for America's food dollar. Competition is increasing and is coming from without as well as from within the industry. In other words, the rapid increase in number and size of conventional supermarkets has led to situations whereby many of these stores are operating below capacity. Dollar sales, sales per square foot, sales per employee, sales per checkout, and many of the other ratios used to view the efficiency of supermarkets have generally declined for stores opened during the past few years. Other problems which may not bode well in terms of continued supermarket growth and expansion remain to be discussed. These include present and continued difficulties in the areas of finance and managerial personnel.

---

[21] "Are Government Commissaries Draining Supermarket Dollars?" *Food Topics,* April, 1961, p. 8.

Financing—Supermarket Dilemma

When food industry executives and trade association officials are polled as to what they consider to be the major problems facing supermarket operations in the future, the overwhelming number of responses fall into two distinct categories. One group argues that securing adequate capital for financing growth and expansion is the biggest problem. The other group replies that hiring and maintaining qualified managerial personnel constitutes the biggest problem. As a matter of fact, private discussions with food executives and an analysis of trade meeting agendas would lead one to believe that these are the *only two* problems facing the industry—prices, rising margins, increased competition, all appear to be overshadowed by these two problems.

Those executives associated with independents or smaller chains tended to stress financing as the biggest problem, and those executives more closely identified with the larger chains tended to stress the managerial problem with the greatest frequency. This is not surprising in light of the characteristics of these two types of operations.

The independent and small chain supermarkets appear to have had the greatest difficulty in obtaining expansion capital. Conventional lending institutions have looked somewhat askance at the supermarket industry as a good field for investment because of low profit margins and rising expenses.[22]

Many smaller-scale supermarket chains and independents have resorted to public financing, such as the sale of stocks and bonds to customers.[23] Some affiliated independents have been able to obtain financing from sponsoring wholesalers, but, generally, this amounts only to working capital and not expansion funds.[24]

Perhaps the growth of some supermarkets has been impeded as a result of being unable to obtain expansion capital, and this condition may continue into the future. However, in light of the present overexpanded condition of the industry, this may be something of a blessing.

---

[22] See "Financial Experts' View of Food Chain Stocks," *Progressive Grocer*, April, 1966, p. 115, and "Private Bear Market," *Forbes*, January 15, 1966, p. 44.
[23] "Food for Thought?" *Barron's*, April 11, 1966, pp. 11, 12, 14.
[24] *Ibid.*

The Coming Need for Qualified Managers

The supermarket industry has historically obtained store managers by training and bringing men up through the ranks. However, today's stores, and especially the operation of tomorrow's supermarkets, are calling for a better, more highly trained and qualified store manager. The supermarket manager of a store having less than 10,000 square feet is only a notch or two above the rank-and-file employee. Many men of outstanding managerial capabilities did not gravitate to these positions. In the tightly run, centrally organized and managed chains, outstanding men simply were not needed as store managers. Today's and tomorrow's supermarkets, however, are likely to be much larger than the 10,000-square-foot supers which reigned during the early fifties. Many supers today run far in excess of 25,000 or even as much as 50,000 square feet, though these would be considered exceptionally large stores. The larger stores call for a much different type of managerial talent. Second, in an effort to gain needed flexibility, most of the large chain units today are becoming decentralized businesses. In these units, managers engage in far-reaching forward planning as opposed merely to carrying out directives issued by national or regional headquarters. This again means that qualified managerial talent must be developed from in-rank employees or brought in, either from (1) other managerial positions with competitors, or (2) recruited from colleges and universities. The best long-run solution appears to be the latter. Paradoxically, managerial personnel are becoming increasingly more difficult to find in the rank-and-file employees. This results, undoubtedly, from the low wage rate which often prevails. Low initial wages simply do not offer the incentive to potential managers to wait out the four or five years sacking groceries and stocking shelves which is necessary as a management apprentice. A higher general wage rate in the industry would probably tend to increase sharply the wage ratio which is already discussed as a major contributory factor to rising expenses and gross margins.[25]

---

[25] For a comprehensive discussion of this problem, see, Douglas Basil, "What Kind of People Will You Find," *A View to 1970: A Five Year Look Ahead*, Super Market Institute, Proceedings of the 1965 Mid-Year Conference, pp. 42-46.

In the long run, the number of managers that can successfully be pirated from others is probably limited. Various stores cannot "steal" managers indefinitely from each other and hope to be benefited as a result of the action.

Therefore, the best solution for the industry would appear to be the initiation of more formal procedures for attracting, training, and holding on to competent talent at the store-manager level. As store size continues to increase, and decentralized organizations become even more the rule rather than the exception, supermarket manager-ship positions should become both more attractive and remunerative.

Many organizations, foreseeing the future difficulties in terms of managerial talent, have started aggressively to recruit college and university graduates for management training programs and intern-ships.[26] Some organizations are anxious to offer part-time work to college and university students in the hope that they may become enamoured with the supermarket business and thus aspire to man-agement positions.[27]

From another point of view, it may very well be that present existing management at both the store and corporate level, given the rapidly accelerating technology, is not maintaining the proper state of readiness for really expert management performance. Or-ganizational innovations, systems analysis, and computer technology have invaded many supermarket operations. Yet the degree to which these technological changes have been assimilated and incorporated as a part of the manager's skill and knowledge is limited. There appears to be a growing isolation of top management away from the mainstream of development. Supermarket management must become involved in the understanding as well as the application and use of this new technology.[28]

One study shows that the supermarket industry has been negli-gent in its responsibility to project the desirable job opportunity "image" in terms of communicating managerial qualifications, salar-

[26] James T. Wyman, "The 'People' Responsibility of Management," *1966 Mid-Year Executive Conference*, National-American Wholesale Grocer's Association, September 7-10, 1966, pp. 15-17.

[27] Douglas Basil, *op. cit.*, p. 43.

[28] Thomas L. Whisler, "Will You Be Qualified To Hold Your Present Job in 1970?" *A View to 1970: A Five Year Look Ahead*, Super Market Institute, Proceedings of the 1965 Mid-Year Conference, pp. 38-41.

ies, and working conditions. The supermarket industry has intoned for a quarter of a century that "people are our most important asset." However, existing management has largely focused on technical competence and forgotten people. Now, the increasing complexity of the supermarket business demands better-qualified management people in rapidly increasing numbers. Unfortunately, food store management has a somewhat jaded image, and this is likely to hamstring it in its efforts to compete for the dwindling supply of available talent. The need for increasing emphasis on management recruitment and development is crucial.[29]

The problem of future shortages of qualified managerial personnel for supermarkets may be alleviated by two conditions:

1. An aggressive, formal, well-organized recruitment and training program.
2. Better financial incentives for potential managerial personnel.

The Supermarket Continues during the Decade of the Seventies

The Supermarket Adapts

Thus far, many problems have been posed which confront the continued growth and development of the supermarket during the seventies. However, surely, this is not the first time the supermarket has been beset by problems and threatened by new forms of competition. Supermarkets have adapted to new forms of competition and to changes in the business environment, and have met changes in other variables in the following ways:

1. *Vertical integration.* Great efforts have been made and achieved by many supermarkets as a result of extending control back through the various stages in food processing and distribution.
2. *General merchandise retailing.* Expansion into general merchandise lines has greatly diversified the supermarkets' operation, and it has enabled them to increase their profit from these higher-margin lines.
3. *Miniaturizing.* In an attempt to get even more business away from the smaller clerk-service stores and in some instances to get business that otherwise might be lost, supermarkets have shrunk in size—hence the bantam and drive-in markets.

---

[29] "The Crisis in Management Development," *Food Topics,* Volume 22, No. 1, January, 1967, pp. 9-20.

4. *Personalized supermarketing.* The big chains have waged a continuous battle throughout the 1960's to instill the "human touch" in their retail stores, in an effort to steal business from the independents.

5. *Emulative merchandising.* The independents, both affiliated and unaffiliated, have constantly emulated the big chains in an effort to gain economies and efficiencies within their operations similar to those of the chain groups.

6. *Controlling brands.* By promoting and controlling their own private brands, many supermarket organizations have been able to improve their profit showing and thus enhance their competitive position.

Thus, supermarkets have to a large extent successfully met the competitive elements of the past. What then of the future? Supermarkets must continue to experiment with new developments in essentially two areas if they are to remain the number-one food-retailing institution in the United States. First, supermarkets must begin to place greater emphasis on operating-expense ratios. And second, they must constantly strive to improve their merchandising strategies.

Attempts To Reduce Operating-Expense Ratios

New competitors will continue to invade what was once considered the bailiwick of the supermarket, if costs are not reduced or held steady. In manufacturing facilities, costs are frequently lowered by introducing labor-saving or capital-equipment devices. The introduction and increased use of capital equipment in the supermarket industry holds great promise as a technique for improving operating-expense ratios, and thus increasing efficiency. Automation seems to be a solution to many of the internal-materials-handling problems. The term "automation" is used here to mean the use of machinery, mechanical objects, equipment, or other non-human devices to supplement or supplant the work of people. This equipment may be used on the selling floor or behind the selling scene, as in storage areas. For the supermarket, automation may be a practical answer in both situations. National Cash Register and Sylvania are among the companies developing automated checkouts. These units operate with optical scanners picking up prices from the customers' selections. The prices are imprinted in specially sensitized ink, and the systems work much like check-processing equipment.[30] The days of queuing in long lines behind a conventional check-out stand may be numbered.

Materials handling in supermarkets is very much undeveloped and offers great potential for improved efficiency and cost reduction. In its handling problems, the supermarket is basically a warehousing function. There is little or no processing, or converting, of raw or semifinished materials in the supermarket. Most of the operations involve receiving, sorting, checking and marking, storage, order picking, order assembling, packing, shipping, and delivery. Consequently, one can see that if these functions can be mechanized, economies may be realized to reduce substantially the materials-handling costs. In food distribution, the great warehouses of the major chains are more widely automated than in other types of retailing. Narrow margins in the supermarket industry will continue to compel these firms to research and investigate the possibilities for increased mechanization and automation in this area. Practically all central warehouses for food chains provide for bulk-palletized storage via fork-lift trucks, controls on stock levels and ordering by tabulating equipment, drag lines, and automatic switching devices, conveyors, and other adjuncts to moving merchandise. Most of the mechanization, however, is applicable to standard grocery items which come in cans or boxes and in standard packs. Handling of produce, fresh meats, dairy products, frozen foods, or the nongrocery items that are increasing in importance is still a major source of difficulty, and still largely unmechanized.[31]

The Penn Fruit Company warehouse is an example of a high degree of automation, but even more importantly, it is an example of the "systems approach" to materials handling. The design is organized around layout rather than automation. The designer based his system on an analysis of sales, product by product and brand by brand. Fast sellers were put near the shipping docks; slow ones to the rear of the building. Thus, types of goods might be split. For

---

[30] E. B. Weiss, "What Will Retailing Be Like in 1975?" *Advertising Age,* March 7, 1966, pp. 119-122.

[31] For some excellent examples and discussion of automation see, John S. Ewing, "Impact of Automation on United States Retail Food Distribution," *Journal of Retailing,* Spring, 1965, pp. 38-47.

example, a popular brand of corn would be placed nearer the door
than a brand that moves slowly. The result creates problems of location which are beyond human memory. All orders must be converted to pick tickets which specify location and quantity and are
arranged in proper sequence.[32]

Significant economies and reductions in handling and order
costs are reported by some firms that are experimenting and adopting various mechanized, or at least simplified, stocking devices for
retail store units. The nearest thing to an automatic stocking device
is a gravity feeding system developed by the Grand Union supermarket organization. This is a display arrangement which is inclined
downward so that merchandise can be fed into the display from
the back by means of the force of gravity. Grand Union is also
experimenting with inclined display shelves with rollers on them
to keep merchandise down forward on the shelves.[33]

Tray packing, which is the stocking and merchandising of canned goods in food stores by utilizing the original shipping carton
as a part of the display, is advocated by some companies as a significant technique for reducing materials handling and labor costs.
The merchandise is generally stacked or shelved in whole-case lots
by utilizing the bottom of the carton as a part of the display.
Many manufacturers are packaging merchandise in special cartons
which have tear strings which facilitate the removal of the excess
protective part of the package.[34] A number of operational advantages are listed for tray-pack stocking. One midwestern firm
lists reduction of shelf inventory without the use of dummies,
better order control and order writing, reduction in inventory-
taking time, faster building of displays, and easier stock rotation
as economies to be gained from using tray pack.[35] Generally, however, tray packs can only be confined to traditionally fast movers
such as canned milk, soup, canned dog food, canned juices and
fruits, coffee, and cereals.[36]

---

[32] Archie J. McGill, "Your Computer, Your Competition and You," *A View to 1970: A Five Year Look Ahead,* Super Market Institute, Proceedings of the 1965 Mid-Year Conference, pp. 30-37.

[33] *Ibid.*

[34] "Tray Packs: Good or Bad?" *Super Market Merchandising,* June, 1960, p. 73.

[35] "Change to Tray Pack Speeds Stocking and Ordering at Marsh," *Chain Store Age,* January, 1960, pp. 80-82.

[36] "Tray Packs: Good or Bad?" *op. cit.*

Methods of stocking shelves vary with different companies, but the principal problems remain much the same. Full displays are needed, shelf and commodity prices must correspond, merchandise must be rotated, and shelves must be kept clean. Whether these duties are accomplished during or after store hours is a matter of company policy. Until about 1957, the tendency was to employ off-hour stocking as store size increased to $20,000 per week and over. The larger the store, the greater the likelihood that night stocking was used. Recently, many supermarkets using night stocking have discontinued the practice and now use day stocking regardless of the store size. Employees engaged in stocking can thus be shifted to checker, bagger, and carry-out assignments during periods of heavy traffic. Undoubtedly, though, some firms may continue to discover economies from night rather than daytime stocking.

The completely automated store is not only feasible but is, right now, a reality. Many firms are now exploring the potential for automatic grocery vending. In densely populated apartment or recreational areas, automatic vending has definite possibilities.[37] Banks of vending machines in small buildings adjacent to suburbs, recreational sites, or for off-hour selling in commercial shopping districts may some day account for a significant proportion of the consumer's fill-in or convenience items. The advent of the change maker has alleviated some of the problems connected with vending distribution. Perhaps very soon now, vending machines will be equipped to handle credit cards, and this may afford even greater opportunities for vending-machine sales.

Several recent accounting innovations are gradually working their way into the supermarket's operations. One of these newer techniques is Expense Center Accounting, an innovation of the mid-1950's. Together with the somewhat related concept of Production Unit Accounting, it represents the first major advance in retail store expense management in more than a quarter of a century.[38]

---

[37] Alan R. Andreasen, "Automated Grocery Shopping," *Journal of Marketing,* Vol. 26, No. 4, October, 1962, p. 64.

[38] Kenneth J. Bauer, "What's in Expense Center Accounting for Retail Stores?" *NACA Bulletin,* March, 1956, pp. 874 ff.

The basic purposes of Expense Center Accounting are to provide a practical arrangement of expense accounts in retail stores that will afford a better understanding of operating costs, facilitate control over the expense structure as a whole, and improve profits. The new system also seeks to eliminate the growing dissatisfaction with the earlier functional groupings of expenses and to provide a satisfactory method of determining the cost of performing particular jobs so that remedial action can be taken where warranted.[39]

Production Unit Accounting and Expense Center Accounting are closely related because their basic purposes are in general the same— to afford a better understanding of operating costs, to facilitate control over expenses, and to improve profits. But whereas the Expense Center concept aims specifically at identifying the principal tasks in retail stores and the costs of performing them, Production Unit Accounting is concerned with the measurement of productivity and the evaluation of performance in relation to those expense centers where it is applicable.[40]

Both these concepts have already been widely adopted by department store firms, and supermarkets are beginning to look more favorably on these devices as means of increasing store control and raising profits.[41]

There can be little doubt that as operating-expense ratios continue to increase and squeeze profit margins, supermarket firms will look more strongly toward labor-saving devices and the increased use of better, more scientific, techniques as the means of reducing operating expenses.

The extent to which automation could be applied to the supermarket is nearly unlimited. Perhaps even the fully automated store may someday become a reality. Customers may ride on moving aisles past the merchandise gondolas. As items strike their fancy, customers will insert a coded tag in a slot below each item. At the

---

[39] National Retail Merchants Association, Controller's Congress, *Standard Expense Center Accounting Manual* (New York: The Association, 1954), pp. 100-110.

[40] *Ibid.*, p. 101. "Expense Center Accounting has to do with the arrangement of the data and its grouping into certain expense centers: whereas Production Unit Accounting is a philosophy for making use of the figures beyond their accumulation into the respective expense centers."

[41] J. P. Deluca, "Space Yield Findings on Cigarettes," *Chain Store Age* (Supermarket Executives Edition), January, 1965, pp. 85-88.

end of the tour, their choices are conveyed to the automated check-out from a behind-the-scenes storeroom.[42] Some time may elapse before customers are ready for this type of de-humanized shopping, but automation may soon result in a more effortless shopping trip for the supermarket customer.

The Need for Improved Merchandising Strategies

The second major method which supermarkets may utilize to maintain their competitive position is to implement changes and experiment with the firm's merchandise mix. Some supermarkets may continue to choose convenience as the primary basis of their appeal. Thus, these stores will offer wide assortments of goods and services. Other firms may choose to compete with a more-vigorous price appeal, and they may further strive to project this price image via an aggressive advertising campaign. Integration may also continue to be explored as a means of increasing operating and merchandising effectiveness. The particular manner in which a firm decides to execute its merchandising strategy and the particular concentration of variables the firm employs will largely determine its success or failure in the market place.

Without changing basic techniques of operation, the supermarket will continue to experiment with elements of the merchandising strategy. A number of scholarly studies have been undertaken in a number of important areas which hold some promise of increasing the effectiveness of the supermarket's selling task. New store designs and layouts are proving to stimulate customers, sales, and profits.[43] Increasing attention is being devoted to such areas as departmentalization of general merchandise lines, concepts of low-center perishables areas, and general store layout.[44] An extensive study of layout, design, and operations of supermarkets was undertaken by Loewy Associates for the Super Market Institute. Many of these recommendations and findings have yet to be incorporated into the supermarkets' merchandising strategies.[45]

---

[42] E. B. Weiss, "What Will Retailing Be Like in 1975?" *op. cit.*, pp. 119-122.

[43] "Store Layout Breakthrough," *Chain Store Age*, December, 1965, p. 48.

[44] "Dimension Added to X-Layout Design," *Progressive Grocer*, December, 1965, p. 74.

[45] See the *Loewy Repo.. to The Super Market Institute*, Loewy Associates, 1961.

The management of grocery inventories and space allocation within the total store area, as well as space allocation among products for various departments, is receiving more and more attention by supermarket operators, academicians, and government agencies.[46] Determinate solutions have yet to be reached in regard to these concepts, but more and more insight is being obtained. Surely, as more of these studies are conducted, supermarket managers will be aided in these space-allocation and inventory-management decisions by more systematic and scientific techniques. The use of statistical and mathematical models holds great promise as an aid to decision making for the supermarket manager in regard to managing the store's inventories.[47]

Supermarket managers will continue to experiment with various promotional devices for increasing store sales volume. Whether double stamp days are more effective than general price cuts has yet to be settled.[48] And for that matter, there are few, if any, "tried and proven" elements to the supermarket merchandising mix.

Discount food merchandisers have set into motion two forces in the field of supermarketing. First, there will be large numbers of conventional food supermarket operators who will rush to get into this new venture. As a matter of fact, large numbers of conventional operators have already found some means of either adapting present facilities to discounting or opening up branches or purchased units which they run as subsidiary discount stores.

The second effect of discount merchandising is somewhat more complex, has far more implications, and may generally have more disruptive effects on the whole field of retail merchandising. As was previously mentioned, much excess capacity already exists in the retail supermarket field. Unused capacity in food retailing generally results in many of the same conditions as excess capacity in a manufacturing enterprise: lower productivity, reduced efficiency, and something less than optimum performance. When conventional

---

[46] Notable among these studies, but far too numerous to list, however, are the many monographs and bulletins of the United States Department of Agriculture.

[47] Edgar A. Pessemier, *The Management of Grocery Inventories in Supermarkets,* Economic and Business Studies, Bulletin No. 32 (Pullman, Washington: Washington State University, April, 1960).

[48] "To Drop or Keep Stamps? Debaters Agree It Depends," *Super Market News,* September 27, 1965, p. 32.

supermarket firms, faced with problems of unused capacity, are all confronted with the additional frustration of competitive inroads from discount supers, the effects on gross margins and, in turn, profits are likely to be severe. Supermarkets have a relatively high ratio of fixed to variable costs, one writer stating that fixed or discretionary fixed costs may constitute 90 per cent of the total cost structure over and above costs of goods sold.[49] Thus, as the discount supers add to an already bloated capacity situation and drain off additional volume from their conventional competitors, the result must logically lead to continuing shrinkage of super-market profit margins and an accelerated mortality rate for marginal supermarket firms.

One likely retaliatory action of the conventional supermarket is to continue "robbing" merchandise lines from other retail groups. Given the relatively high proportion of fixed costs, adequate volume over which to spread this fixed cost becomes an absolute necessity for the supermarket. Consequently, discount food merchandisers are likely to have much of a disruptive effect in the entire retail industry, causing something of a state of disequilibrium. When the supermarket attempts to recoup volume by robbing other retail lines, several merchandising tactics are likely to emerge. Much of the supermarkets' nonfood activities will center around "in-and-out promotions," *i.e.*, promoting general merchandise lines on a "one-shot" basis or promoting highly seasonal items, such as nursery items, garden supplies, seasonal hardware items, and other lines for short periods each year.

Unquestionably, the supermarket will continue to explore opportunities for raiding merchandise lines in soft-goods categories, traffic appliances, and other merchandise lines which lend themselves to supermarket selling techniques. Therefore, the longer-run consequences are significant to the smaller variety, hardware, and junior department stores which are frequently higher margin operations and can ill afford significant losses of volume. This condition

---

[49] Bob R. Holdren, *The Structure of a Retail Market and the Market Behavior of Retail Units* (Englewood Cliffs, New Jersey: Prentice-Hall, Inc., 1960), pp. 29-40.

tends to enhance the generally higher mortality rate of small retailers and the ratio of creditor losses.[50]

In light of these developments, one caveat appears foremost for the supermarket industry: efficiency and productivity must be improved and operating margins reduced. Some hope appears in the offing to enable the industry to accomplish these goals, but time is of the essence. The lag between theoretical developments which lead to better tools and better methods for controlling operations must be narrowed. A whole host of new developments awaits the supermarket operator for his experimentation, development, and adoption.[51]

The potential for grocery store sales in 1975 is something approaching $110 billion. Certainly there are many who are anxious to get and increase their share of this potential during this decade; drive-in markets, case-lot wholesalers, commissaries, and discounters are a few of these competitors. Many conventional supermarket merchants will move rapidly to discount merchandising. Others will attempt to compete via strategies and tactics other than price. However, one reasonable assumption appears to be that mass merchandising via self-service and cash-and-carry policies will continue as the dominant food-retailing feature in 1975.

Summary

The supermarket, in spite of some competitive inroads, will remain in all likelihood the dominant retail food institution throughout the decade of the 1970's. Prospects appear quite good that retail grocery store sales will reach $110 billion by 1975. However, there are several challengers for this lucrative market. Some forces are at work which could completely unsettle the entire super-

---

[50] Rom J. Markin, "The Demise of the Marginal Retailing Establishment," *Journal of Retailing*, Vol. 43, No. 2, Summer, 1967, pp. 28-38.

[51] A complete analysis and description of these developments and techniques is beyond the scope of this discussion. However, without further embellishments, several of these techniques and developments can be found in the following. See William S. Peters, "Control of Stocks in Grocery Retailing," *The Journal of Marketing* (October, 1957), pp. 148-153. F. E. Balderston, "Assortment Choices in Wholesale and Retail Marketing," *The Journal of Marketing* (October, 1956), pp. 175-183. Wayne A. Lee, "Space Management in Retail Stores and Implications to Agriculture," *Marketing Keys to Profits in the 1960's*, American Marketing Association, 1960, pp. 523-533. John F. Magee, *Production Planning and Inventory Control*, McGraw-Hill Book Company, New York, 1958. Robert G. Brown, *Statistical Forecasting for Inventory Control*, McGraw-Hill Book Company, New York, 1959.

market industry. Notable among these challengers are the discount food merchandisers, the case-lot sellers, and the drive-in markets. An extremely critical problem of supermarkets, one for which there appear few immediate solutions, is that of the constantly rising operating-expense ratios and the consequently increased gross margins of supermarkets. Supermarket managers are looking in two directions toward the solution to this problem. First, increasing attention is being placed on controlling expenses via the introduction of labor-saving capital equipment and, by adopting generally, more scientific devices into the supermarket operation. Second, the supermarket managers are constantly experimenting with various elements of the merchandising mix. The supermarket is still primarily a merchandising establishment, and the industry must continue to attract large numbers of customers into its stores. Perhaps the greatest challenge facing the conventional supermarket operator is that of the discount food merchandisers. The methods of the discounters are likely to alter conventional supermarket merchandising strategies and techniques significantly. However, the basic techniques of food retailing in 1975 will undoubtedly be self-service and cash-and-carry merchandising. These, of course, are the basic techniques of the present-day supermarket.

* BIBLIOGRAPHY

Books

Baranoff, Seymour. "Retailing as an Operating System," *Theory in Marketing,* Reavis Cox, Wroe Alderson, and Stanley Shapiro (eds.), 2nd Series (Homewood, Illinois: Richard D. Irwin, Inc., 1964).

Boyd, Harper, and Sidney J. Levy. *Promotion: A Behavioral View* (Englewood Cliffs, New Jersey: Prentice-Hall, Inc., 1967).

Brown, Robert G. *Statistical Forecasting for Inventory Control* (New York: McGraw-Hill Book Company, 1959).

Charvat, Frank J. *Supermarketing* (New York: The MacMillan Co., 1960).

Duncan, Delbert J., and Charles F. Phillips. *Retailing: Principles and Methods* (Homewood, Illinois: Richard D. Irwin, Inc., 1967).

Entenberg, R. D. *Effective Retail and Market Distribution* (New York: The World Publishing Company, 1966).

Goodwin, Arthur E. *Markets Public and Private* (Seattle, Washington: Montgomery Printing Company, 1939).

Hall, Margaret. *Distributive Trading* (London: Hutchinson's University Library, 1949).

Haring, Albert, and Wallace O. Yoder (eds.). *Trading Stamp Practice and Pricing Policy* (Bloomington, Indiana: Bureau of Business Research, School of Business, Indiana University, 1958).

Holdren, Bob R. *The Structure of a Retail Market and the Market Behavior of Retail Units* (Englewood Cliffs, New Jersey: Prentice-Hall, Inc., 1960).

Howard, John A. *Marketing Management: Analysis and Decision,* rev. ed. (Homewood, Illinois: Richard D. Irwin, Inc., 1953).

Kuznets, Simon. *Shares of Upper Income Groups in Income and Savings* (New York: National Bureau of Economic Research, Inc., 1953).

Lebhor, Godfrey M. *Chain Stores in America* (New York: Chain Store Publishing Company, 1959).

[157]

Magee, John F. *Production Planning and Inventory Control* (New York: McGraw-Hill Book Company, 1958).

Oxenfeldt, Alfred R. "The Formulation of a Market Strategy," *Managerial Marketing: Perspectives and Viewpoints*. E. Kelly and W. Lazar (eds.) (Homewood, Illinois: Richard D. Irwin, Inc., 1958).

Phillips, Charles F., and Delbert J. Duncan. *Marketing Principles and Methods* (Homewood, Illinois: Richard D. Irwin, Inc., 1956).

Smith, Henry. *Retail Distribution*, 1st ed. (London: Oxford University Press, 1937).

Stigler, George J. *Five Lectures on Economic Problems* (New York: The MacMillan Company, 1950).

Weimer, Arthur M., and Homer Hoyt. *Principles of Real Estate*, 3rd ed. (New York: The Ronald Press Company, 1954).

Wingate, J. W., and E. O. Scholler. *Techniques of Retail Merchandising* (New York: Prentice-Hall, Inc., 1950).

Zimmerman, M. M. *The Super Market: A Revolution in Distribution* (New York: McGraw-Hill Book Company, Inc., 1955).

Periodicals

Adams, Kendall A. "Achieving Market Organization through Voluntary and Cooperative Groups," *Journal of Retailing* (Summer, 1966).

Andreasen, Alan R. "Automated Grocery Shopping," *Journal of Marketing* (October, 1962).

Applebaum, William. "Guidelines for a Store-Location Strategy Study," *Journal of Marketing* (October, 1966).

Applebaum, William, and Saul B. Cohen. "Store Trading Areas in a Changing Market," *Journal of Retailing* (Fall, 1961).

Balderston, F. E. "Assortment Choices in Wholesale and Retail Marketing," *Journal of Marketing* (October, 1956).

Bonwich, William. "Study of General Merchandise," *Food Topics* (March, 1960).

Boyd, Harper W., Jr., and Ronald Frank. "The Importance of Private Labels in Food Retailing," *Business Horizons* (Summer, 1966).

Bunck, Gilbert. "What Makes Women Buy?" *Fortune* (August, 1956).

Cassady, R., Jr., and R. M. Williams. "Radio as an Advertising Medium," *Harvard Business Review* (January, 1949).

Converse, Paul D. "Twenty-Five Years of Wholesaling—A Revolution in Food Wholesaling," *Journal of Marketing* (July, 1957).

Deluca, J. P. "Space Yield Findings on Cigarettes," *Chain Store Age*, Supermarket Executives Edition (January, 1965).

Dichter, Ernest. "The Point of Point of Purchase," *Food Marketing* (May-June, 1954).

Ewing, John S. "Impact of Automation on United States Retail Food Distribution," *Journal of Retailing* (Spring, 1965).

Flint, Lucius S. "The Los Angeles Super," *Chain Store Age* (June, 1950).

Harrison, J. S. "Self-Service—A Development of the Machine Age," *Chain Store Age* (May, 1939).

Hauser, Phillip M. "The Challenge of Tomorrow's Markets," *Journal of Marketing* (July, 1959).

Hollander, Stanley C. "Notes on the Retail Accordion," *Journal of Retailing* (Summer, 1966).

Holton, Richard H. "Price Discrimination at Retail: The Supermarket Case," *The Journal of Industrial Economics* (October, 1957).

Hood, Julia, and B. S. Yamey. "Imperfect Competition in the Retail Trades," *Economica* (1951).

Kaylin, S. O. 27th Annual *Chain Store Age* Survey of Construction and Modernization, *Chain Store Age,* Supermarket Executives Edition (January, 1966).

Kollat, David T., and Ronald P. Willett. "Consumer Impulse Purchasing Behavior," *Journal of Marketing Research* (February, 1967).

LaLonde, B. J. "New Frontiers in Store Location," *Supermarket Merchandising* (February, 1963).

Linden, Fabian. "Family Formation," *The Conference Board Record,* The National Industrial Conference Board, Inc. (February, 1967).

Linden, Fabian. "The Nation's Marketplace in 1975 . . . Growing Younger and Richer," *The Conference Board Record,* The National Industrial Conference Board, Inc. (May, 1967).

Main, Jeremy. "A Slow Getaway for the Auto Market," *Fortune* (June 1, 1967).

Markin, Rom J. "The Demise of the Marginal Retailing Establishment," *Journal of Retailing* (Summer, 1967).

Markin, Rom J. "The Superette: Opportunity for the Independent Owner," *Journal of Retailing* (Spring, 1963).

Mayer, Laurence A. "Why the U. S. Population Isn't Exploding," *Fortune* (April, 1967).

Manichiello, Robert J. "The Real Challenge of Food Discounters," *Journal of Marketing* (April, 1967).

Pessemier, Edgar A. "Applying Supermarket Techniques to Non-Food Retailing," *Journal of Retailing* (Summer, 1960).

Peters, William S. "Control of Stocks in Grocery Retailing," *Journal of Marketing* (October, 1957).

Settel, Irving. "Why Retailers Bypass Television," *Journal of Retailing* (Winter, 1955-1956).

Smith, Paul E. "Merchandising for the Teen Age Market," *Journal of Retailing* (Summer, 1961).

Stolnitz, George J. "Our Growing Population: Threat or Boon," *Business Horizons* (Summer, 1959).

Twedt, D. W. "Does the '9-Fixation' in Retailing Pricing Really Promote Sales?" *Journal of Marketing* (October, 1964).

Udell, Jon G. "Can Attitude Measurement Predict Consumer Behavior?" *Journal of Marketing* (October, 1965).

Weiss, E. B. "What Will Retailing Be Like in 1975?" *Advertising Age* (March 7, 1966).

ANONYMOUS

"A New Dimension: Economic and Marketing Geography," *Food Topics* (March, 1961).

"A Statistical Profile of the Modern Super Market—The Colonial Study," *Progressive Grocer* (October, 1963).

"Are Government Commissaries Draining Supermarket Dollars?" *Food Topics* (April, 1961).

"The Art of Locating New Stores Seen Fast Becoming a Science: SMI Annual Convention," *Super Market News* (May 17, 1965).

"Change to Tray Pack Speeds Stocking and Ordering at Marsh," *Chain Store Age* (January, 1960).

"The Cheapy Thrives," *Business Week* (February 8, 1933).

"Colonial Study Data Can Help Improve Store Operation," *Progressive Grocer* (November, 1963).

"The Crisis in Management Development," *Food Topics* (January, 1967).

"Data Processing," *Super Market News* (October 18, 1965).

"The Dillon Study," *Progressive Grocer* (June, 1960), (October, 1960).

"Dimension Added to X-Layout Design," *Progressive Grocer* (December, 1965).

"Do Games Pay Off?" *Super Market News* (June 21, 1965).

"Emphasis Shifts to the Selling Committees," *Progressive Grocer* (June, 1959).

Facts in Grocery Distribution, 28th Annual Survey, *Progressive Grocer* (April, 1961).

"Financial Experts' View of Food Chain Stocks," *Progressive Grocer* (April, 1966).

"Five Ways Stores Are Combating New Competition," *Chain Store Age* (May, 1965).

"Food for Thought?" *Barron's* (April 11, 1966).

"Food Report Feeds Controversy," *Business Week* (May 28, 1966).

"Food Retailing—A Restless, Ever-Changing Business," *Progressive Grocer* (October, 1952).

"Food Retailing 1975—A Look into the Future," *Progressive Grocer* (April, 1966).

"Food Retailing Weathers Stormy Year with Best Sales Gains in Decade," Thirty-Fourth Annual Report of the Grocery Industry, *Progressive Grocer* (April, 1967).

"The Food Town Study," *Progressive Grocer* (January, 1955).

"Handbill Advertising Brings 11% Volume Gain," *Progressive Grocer* (January, 1960).

"High Court Bars Merger of Rivals," *Business Week* (June 4, 1966).

"How an Average Customer Spends Her Super Market Dollars—Super Value Markets," *Facts in Grocery Distribution,* 26th Annual Survey, *Progressive Grocer* (April, 1959).

"How Much Do Customers Know about Retail Prices," *Progressive Grocer* (February, 1964).

"Improving Sale Item Display: The Display and Merchandising Workshop," *Chain Store Age* (January, 1965).

"Looking Backwards: 25 Years of Super Market Progress," *Super Market Merchandising* (August, 1955).

"The Lush New Suburban Market," *Fortune* (November, 1953).

"Neilson Surveys Food Discounting," *Super Market Merchandising* (January, 1965).

"New Products: $11 Billion New Business since 1954," *Progressive Grocer* (April, 1965).

"Non-Food Notes," *Super Market Merchandising* (November, 1955).

"Now Image plus Price Appeal," *Chain Store Age* (June, 1965).

"Once-a-Week Label Introduction," *Super Market News* (February 1, 1960).

"Own Label Additions Slated by 19% in Poll," *Super Market News* (August 1, 1960).

"Private Bear Market," *Forbes* (January 15, 1966).

"Private Labels Termed Sales Asset," *Super Market News* (February 29, 1960).

"Promote the Whole Store," *Food Merchandising* (April, 1960).

"Report of the A.M.A. Definition Committee," *Journal of Marketing* (October, 1948).

"Self-Service Layout Boosts Unit Sales from 72¢ to $1.60," *Progressive Grocer* (October, 1929).

"Shelf Altitudes Affect Buying Attitudes," *Progressive Grocer* (March, 1964).

"Small Size . . . Big Success," *Food Topics* (April, 1965).

"Some Real Estate Considerations," *Super Market Merchandising* (August, 1959).

"Sophistication in Supermarkets: Rack Jobbers Polish Technique," *Merchandising Week* (November 8, 1965).

"Store Layout Breakthrough," *Chain Store Age,* Grocery Executives Edition (December, 1965).

"The Story of the Food Chains," *Chain Store Age,* Grocery Executives Edition (June, 1950).

"Super Market Site Selection Today's Tough Decision: SMI," *Super Market News* (November 22, 1965).

Thirty-Fourth Annual Report of the Grocery Industry, *Progressive Grocer* (April, 1967).

"To Drop or Keep Stamps? Debaters Agree It Depends," *Supermarket News* (September 27, 1965).

"Tray Packs: Good or Bad?" *Super Market Merchandising* (June, 1960).

"Two Chains Try Vest Pocket Centers," *Chain Store Age* (March 1, 1967).

"U.S. Consumer Products Rack Up New Advance in Operating Results," *Barron's* (August 23, 1965).

"The Uses of Aerial Photography," *Super Market Merchandising* (May, 1960).

"Wall Street Says," *Super Market Merchandising* (August, 1965).

"Where Sales and Profits Come From—The Dillon Company," *Progressive Grocer* (1960).

"Where We Stand Today in Private Brand Merchandising," *Progressive Grocer* (August, 1959).

"Wholesale Success: Incentive Plus Service Adds Up to Profits for Voluntary Food Merchants," *Barron's* (July 4, 1966).

Miscellaneous

Basil, Douglas. "What Kind of People Will You Find," *A View to 1970: A Five Year Look Ahead,* Super Market Institute, Proceedings of the 1965 Mid-Year Conference.

Bureau of Advertising, American Newspaper Publishers Association, Inc., 1965, in Otto Kleppner, *Advertising Procedure,* 5th ed. (Englewood Cliffs, New Jersey: Prentice-Hall, Inc., 1966).

"The Changing Times," *Proceedings of the Mid-Year Conference,* Super Market Institute (January, 1962).

Cole *et al. Manufacturer and Distributor Brands,* Bulletin Series: No. 80 (Urbana, Illinois: University of Illinois, 1955).

"The Colonial Study," *Progressive Grocer* (1963-1964).

"Consumer Dynamics in the Super Market," *Progressive Grocer,* Parts I-VI (October, 1965-March, 1966).

"Facts about New Super Markets Opened in 1965," *Eighteenth Annual Report,* Super Market Institute, 1966.

The Fortune Directory of the 500 Largest U.S. Industrial Corporations, Editors of *Fortune, Fortune* (July 15, 1966).

Fox, Karl A. *The Analysis of Demand for Farm Products,* U.S. Department of Agriculture Technical Bulletin 1081 (Washington: U.S. Government Printing Office, 1953).

Hauser, Phillip M. "Is the Market Moving Away from You?" *A View to 1970,* Super Market Institute Proceedings of the 1965 Mid-Year Conference.

The Housewife and the Food Industry (New York: Kenyon and Eckhart, Inc., 1960).

Lee, Wayne A. "Space Management in Retail Stores and Implications to Agriculture," *Marketing Keys to Profits in the 1960's* (Chicago: American Marketing Association, 1960).

Life Study of Consumer Expenditures (New York: Time, Inc., 1957).

Loewy Report to the Super Market Institute, Loewy Associates (1961).

McGill, Archie J. "Your Computer, Your Competition and You," *A View to 1970: A Five Year Look Ahead,* Super Market Institute, Proceedings of the 1965 Mid-Year Conference.

"Organization and Competition in Food Retailing," Technical Study No. 7, National Commission on Food Marketing (June, 1966).

Pessemier, Edgar A. *The Management of Grocery Inventories in Supermarkets,* Economic and Business Studies, Bulletin No. 32 (Pullman, Washington: Washington State University, 1960).

Quinn, William J. "Advertising in Action," Summary Report NAFC Management Clinic, *Sales Promotion and Advertising* (January, 1955).

Smith, A. B. (ed.). "Significant Trends and Developments in the Postwar Period," *Competitive Distribution in a Free High-Level Economy and Its Implications for the University* (Pittsburgh: University of Pittsburgh Press, 1958).

Super Market Institute, *Proceedings of the 1965 Mid-Year Conference.*

Super Market Institute, *The Super Market Industry Speaks,* Thirteenth and Eighteenth Annual Reports (Chicago: Super Market Institute, 1961 and 1966).

"The Super Value Study," *Progressive Grocer* (1958).

U.S. Bureau of the Census, *1960 Census of Population,* Vol. I, *Characteristics of the Population,* Part A, Number of Inhabitants (Washington: U.S. Government Printing Office, 1961).

U.S. Circuit Court of Appeals, 7th District, testimony by Malcolm P. McNair, "United States vs. the Great Atlantic and Pacific Tea Company," Docket 9221, *Records and Briefs,* Vol. II.

U.S. Department of Agriculture, Agricultural Marketing Service, *Consumption of Food in the United States, 1909-52.*

U.S. Department of Agriculture, Production and Marketing Administration, Marketing Research Report No. 30, *Better Allocation of Selling Space in Food Stores: Part I—Relation of Size of Display to Sales of Canned Fruits and Vegetables* (Washington: U.S. Government Printing Office, November, 1952).

U.S. Department of Agriculture, Agricultural Marketing Service, Statistical Bulletin No. 364, Supplement, 1965.

U.S. Department of Commerce, Bureau of the Census, *Current Population Reports,* Series P-20, No. 151 and Series P-25, No. 329.

U.S. Department of Commerce, Bureau of the Census, *Number of Inhabitants, U.S. Summary Census of Population* (Washington: U.S. Government Printing Office, 1950).

U.S. Department of Commerce, Bureau of the Census, *Sixteenth Census of the U.S., 1940 Population,* Vol. 1 (Washington: U.S. Government Printing Office, 1942).

U.S. Federal Trade Commission, *Economic Inquiry into Food Marketing,* Part 1 (Washington: U.S. Government Printing Office, 1960).

Wallin, David E. "A Marketing Profile of the Senior Citizen Group," *Marketing's Role in Scientific Management* (Chicago: American Marketing Association, 1957).

Wedding, Nugent. "Contemporary Brand Policies," *Frontiers in Marketing Thought,* contributed papers, conference of the American Marketing Association (Bloomington, Indiana: Indiana University, December, 1954).

Whisler, Thomas L. "Will You Be Qualified To Hold Your Present Job in 1970?" *A View to 1970: A Five Year Look Ahead,* Super Market Institute, Proceedings of the 1965 Mid-Year Conference.

Women Speak Their Minds on Supermarkets. A nationwide survey conducted by the Research Department of Paramount Paper Products, Omaha, Nebraska (1961).

Wyman, James T. "The People: Responsibility of Management," *1966 Mid-Year Executive Conference,* National-American Wholesale Grocer's Association (September 7-10, 1966).